EXPERIENCING GOD

FOSTERING A CONTEMPLATIVE LIFE

DENNIS J. BILLY, C.SS.R.

LIGUORI, MISSOURI

Published by Liguori Publications
Liguori, Missouri
http://www.liguori.org

Library of Congress Cataloging-in-Publication Data

Billy, Dennis Joseph
Experiencing God : fostering a contemplative life / Dennis J. Billy.
p. cm.
ISBN 0-7648-0658-0 (pbk)
1. Spiritual life—Catholic Church. 2. Contemplation. I. Title.

BX2350.2 .B52 2000
248.4'82—dc21 00–029604

Printed in the United States of America
04 03 02 01 00 5 4 3 2 1
First Edition

In memory of Sister Mary Regina, O.Ss.R.
(Helen Smolkovich)
1928–1998

*It is the heart which experiences God,
and not the reason*

BLAISE PASCAL, *PENSÉES*

CONTENTS

ACKNOWLEDGMENTS

Parts of this book have appeared elsewhere under the following titles: "*Lectio Divina:* The Contemplative Reading of God's Word," *Pastoral Life* 47 (no. 11, 1998): 18–22; "The Desert As Spiritual Landscape," *Review for Religious* 57 (1998): 299–303; "Praying the Jesus Prayer," *Pastoral Life* 47 (no. 6, 1998): 36–38; "The Desert in the City," *The Priest* 54 (no 4, 1998): 14–17; "Afraid of Asking: About Petitionary Prayer," *Pastoral Life* 47 (no. 4, 1998): 6–11; "Praying the Psalms," *Pastoral Life* 46 (no. 8, 1997): 11–13; "The Waters of Vaucluse," *Review for Religious* 56 (1997): 182–86; "The Rhythm of Prayer," *Pastoral Life* 46 (no. 2, 1997): 28–33; "Windows for Prayer," *The Priest* 52 (no. 12, 1996): 12–15; "On Praying the Lord's Prayer: A Reflection on Luke 11:1–4," *Pastoral Life* 45 (no. 9, 1996): 37–39; "A Visit to Taizé," *Review for Religious* 55 (1996): 55–60. Special thanks go to the editors and staff of *Pastoral Life, The Priest,* and *Review for Religious* for allowing me to incorporate these pieces into a larger work.

Introduction

At one time or another you probably have been asked if you believe in God and, perhaps, who or what you think God might be like. But have you ever been asked if you have actually experienced God? A question like this is often met with apprehension. It is somehow easier for us to argue about God's existence or speak about the various images we might have of God than to share with others those very personal times when we felt that we may have been touched by the divine. After all, no one wants to be thought of as having a couple of screws loose; no one wants to be dismissed as one of those flighty pseudomystical types who have lost contact with the real world.

This reluctance to speak about experiences of God, however, eventually takes its toll on the human heart. Christianity is all about the human experience of the divine and the divine experience of the human. It is Good News that needs to be shared. It tells us that God has entered our world in the person of Jesus—and refuses to leave it. It tells us that we do not have to leave this world to find God, but that God has left heaven to find us. The Incarnation has changed the way in which God relates to us and to all of creation. Because of Jesus, the Word made flesh (see John 1:14), we can now approach God with both feet planted firmly on the ground. In him, the divine touches us not in some other world for which we were never made and to which we do not belong, but in our homes and workplaces, in our environment, in our friendships and families and, most especially, in the depths of our hearts.

Introduction

You find before you fifteen short reflections—or "books," as I prefer to call them—on how God can be experienced in today's world. These "books" use literature, Christian doctrine, Scripture, nature, personal experience, metaphor, and theological reflection to demonstrate just a few of the ways in which God reveals to us a sense of the divine mystery in the here and now. The purpose of these reflections is not to map out the experience of God, but to stimulate your own thoughts on where and how the divine has manifested itself to you in your own life. In this sense, these reflections are only a point of departure for your own reflections.

Each reflection stands alone (and can be read as such) but is situated in the larger whole to communicate a sense of movement and growth in the spiritual life. Each is introduced by an appropriate quotation, usually a brief poem or a few verses from Scripture, followed by a series of questions carefully designed to guide your subsequent reflection on what it means to foster a contemplative attitude toward life. The exercise following these questions brings each "book" to completion by offering a concrete suggestion for integrating these insights into your daily life of prayer. The two brief excerpts from Thomas Merton's *Seeds of Contemplation* at the beginning and the end of the collection serve as "spiritual bookends" to remind you of some underlying themes that are present throughout.

The purpose of this collection is to nurture in your heart a sense of the great variety of ways in which God speaks to us. This collection cannot give you an experience of God, of course, but it can point you in the right direction and show you what to look for and what to be wary of. It may also help you live with a deeper sense of expectancy for what lies ahead. Other than that, you will be pretty much on your own—although never alone. God seems to want it that way. Half the enjoyment lies in the search; the rest, in coming to the realization that God always meets us where we are—with open, gracious, and ever welcoming arms.

BOOKEND

Our discovery of God is, in a way,
God's discovery of us.
We cannot go to heaven
to find Him
because we have no way
of knowing where heaven is
or what it is.
He comes down from heaven
and finds us.

THOMAS MERTON[1]

Book One

MORNING PRAYERS

Dawn points, and another day
Prepares for heat and silence.
Out at sea the dawn wind
Wrinkles and slides.
I am here
Or there, or elsewhere.
In my beginning.

T. S. ELIOT, "EAST COKER"[2]

Before the break of dawn, as night slowly loosens its hold over the earth and quietly gives way to a dreamy, semiconscious realm of shadow and light, I emerge from the darkness of sleep and enter a momentary mist of silent unknowing. Numb to my whereabouts, I crack open my eyes and gradually distinguish myself from the faint appearances of things in my room. A timer clicks at 5:30 A.M. and the sounds of dripping coffee beat upon my ears—my dilated nostrils sniff out the scent of its full-bodied aroma. I hesitate for a few drowsy moments, not knowing where I am. I wet my lips, taste the thin residue of salt on my skin, then turn over lazily to the other side of my bed. Just as the strums of guitar music filter through my mind, providing a background score for the final scenes of my quickly fading dreams, the radio alarm registers in my mind. With my covers now well up over my head, I extend my arm outward in a halfhearted attempt to locate its whereabouts.

Ever so slowly, awareness enters my world. I lift my head from my pillow, then lay it down again with a slight tinge of regret. Morning has broken. My dreams call out to me, begging me not to leave them behind, but their voices, already faint from the waning night, have long lost their power to persuade. I linger in bed for a few listless moments, then roll over one last time before I grudgingly turn off the alarm.

OUT OF BED

Now comes the easy part. I reach out to turn on a small lamp, throw off my covers and, in one swift motion, find myself sitting in my nightclothes on the side of my bed. Looking down at the floor from my sagging mattress, I slowly run my fingers through my hair and let my hand rest on the nape of my neck. Then, looking up at the ceiling and breathing deeply, yesterday's thoughts invade my mind. I try to ward them off for one last moment but find that I have already succumbed. I close my eyes and release a deep sigh.

In the next moment, I am standing on the cold, tile floor, looking for my slippers and moving my legs up and down to protect my feet from the cold. I shake my head to and fro, releasing a gentle whinny from the vibrations of my cheeks and lips. I find my slippers and put them on, but not before casting one last glance at my empty bed. The new day beckons—but so do the unconscious sirens of the night. I sense a need in me to somehow reconcile the two.

Already the rituals I use to mark the beginning of each new day have taken over. I put on my robe, pour a cup of coffee, sip it leisurely (and in silence), sit down in a chair, and allow my mind to wander. A stream of images flows through me—people, events, places—presenting themselves when they wish and as they wish, with little rhyme or reason. These early morning visitors slowly put me back in touch with the world. I welcome each of them as they come, and I bid them all to sit with me. I am never alone at this early morning hour, not even in the solitude of my own room. There is much to ponder when I allow these quiet companions to speak. They have much to tell and, when I listen, much wisdom to impart.

When I finish my coffee, I wash my face, shave, brush my teeth, comb my hair, and get dressed. All of these actions bear my personal signature: the order and manner in which they are done, the time allotted to each, the importance I place on them. Together they bring a sense of order to the day's beginning and help me make it my own. They are my way of saying to myself, *My presence makes a difference in the world—and the world makes a difference to me.* They help me begin the day with a sense of purpose. In these small, insignificant ways, I set myself apart from the rest of life—and assert my existence.

My Sacred Space

Still half asleep, I make my way to a special corner of my room set aside for prayer. This, too, is one of my waking rituals and bears my personal touch. Each morning at this hour I light a small candle before an icon on the wall. Although all is quiet in this small sacred space, the darkness around me dwindles as the light of day breaks through the window of my room and chirping swallows announce the arrival of dawn. I sit in the shadows with my eyes closed—but I could just as well leave them open. At this early morning hour my inner and outer worlds seem strangely fused.

Time passes: sometimes slowly, sometimes quickly. I take little notice except when I need to crack my neck or shift my weight around on my chair. What is more, I always sit in the same position: upright against the back of my chair with my arms resting in my lap. I do so almost instinctively, without a modicum of forethought or reflection. The sameness and regularity of these actions allow me to blend with my surroundings and be alone, in perfect stillness, with the waning darkness and the silent Other I call God.

It is difficult to describe what I do for the next thirty minutes. In one sense I do very little. I just sit there with my eyes closed, slowly breathing in and out, and trying to be as still as possible. I try not to think but am not always successful. When thoughts get in the way, I recognize them for what they are, accept them, and try to let go of them. To keep me from thinking too much, I have taken to reciting the Jesus Prayer and slowly running my fingers through my prayer beads. "Lord Jesus Christ, have mercy on me. Lord Jesus Christ, have mercy on me." Repeating the same words over and over again has a soothing effect on my soul and enables me to listen more deeply to the inner rhythm of my heart. This is what works for me, at least most of the time. When it doesn't work, I simply stare into the icon. By now, I know every curve and color of the gilded two-dimensional image of the Madonna and Child. I simply gaze into their eyes, and they gaze back at me. It's as simple as that. Nothing more; nothing less. Anyone can do it. Eternity seems closer when I pray this way; it brushes across the canvas of my soul and leaves its image behind. At such moments, my outer world reveals to me my inner world, showing me that I, too, am an icon, a window to eternity that reveals the light of day. When a thought enters my mind, I ponder it, sit with it, and let it go—for now is not a time for thought. That will come later, when the day is further spent and matters of consequence vie for my attention. Now is a time to be still in the presence of God, the silent Other, for whom I so desperately long.

"Out of the depths I cry to you, O Lord." The words form naturally on my lips and come straight from my heart. From the depths of it, the child that I am before the silent Other speaks and is heard. At this moment, nothing else matters. I try not to be conscious of anything, not my thoughts, my breathing, the words I am whispering—not even the beating of my heart. I try to be as consciousless as possible. This is the time simply to be with myself, with the world, with the silent Other. In that silence, I open up to existence and sit with the Ground that sustains it. All the universe resounds in my heart. By probing its depths I find that, in this utter stillness, I can move in and with that which keeps all things in being.

This way of prayer has become so ingrained in me that it seems almost natural. I know, however, that I am not responsible for it; I know that someone else allows it to happen. Such peak experiences do not last long: a moment here, a moment there. Much of my time is spent waiting. Nor does my prayer depend on these peak experiences. The waiting itself is made sacred by the silent Other—and such waiting goes a long way. Even when my stillness is broken by distractions, my peace remains undisturbed. Why? Because I have come to see that everything is grace. All things can lead me to God, if God so wills—and that is all I seek. A sense of gratitude rises up within me. I am alive; I am breathing; I am sitting; I am praying—and none of this has occurred by chance. I am a child of God. I am connected to everything in the universe. "Thank you, Lord, thank you!"

Conclusion

I am startled by a small, beeping sound. Where am I? Where is that sound coming from? Am I still in bed? I must have dozed off. That happens from time to time—at least to me. I come to my senses and realize that my watch alarm is signaling the end of my prayer time. I find the right button, press it, bow my head, and let out a deep, silent sigh. Part of me does not want to move and wishes to extend my prayer a few moments longer. I often do—but not always. Within a short time, I find myself stretching my arms over my head and giving way, yet again, to another spell of early morning yawning. The time is 6:30 A.M.

I make my bed, arrange my room, and get ready for breakfast. As I perform these minor tasks, different people drift through my mind. Some are close friends; some I barely know; some are complete strangers. Whoever they are, I greet them one by one, offer them a place in my heart, and invite them to journey with me for the day. As the sun raises its head above the horizon and streaks of daylight enter my room, I open my door and step out to greet the world.

REFLECTION QUESTIONS

1. How do you normally begin your day? Have you devised any particular routine to help you get started? If so, what is it? (Try to be as specific as possible.) If it helps, make a list of the things you do. Are you happy with your early morning ritual? If so, what do you like about it? If not, what might you do to change it?

2. Does prayer play a role in the way you begin your day? If it does, then describe the particulars of your morning prayer. (Try to be as specific as possible.) Do you have set prayers that you say over and over? Do you talk to God? Do you pray for others? Do you ask for help? Does your prayer involve quiet time? Do you give yourself time to get in touch with the deepest part of yourself?

3. Do you have a sacred space in your life, a particular place in your room or house where you go to become still and centered? If so, where is it? Do you go there often? Do you go there at the beginning of the day? What do you do there? What makes this space special? How does it help you? If you do not have a sacred space, does it make sense for you to create one? If not, why not?

4. Do you feel comfortable being still? Are you able to be still for a few minutes each day? Does it help you to find that sacred place in your heart, where you can rest in the presence of God's Spirit and allow it to groan within you? How else do you collect yourself at the outset of each day?

5. Does your prayer help you in going forth? Does it encourage you to face the responsibilities of the day? Does it enable you to see the hand of God in the various circumstances that come your way throughout the day? Do you see a continuity between your time in prayer and the rest of life? As your prayer life deepened, has it given you any new insights into yourself and others? Has it pointed out any areas in your life that might need changing?

Exercise

Set your alarm so that you will get up half an hour earlier than usual. When you get up the next morning, go to the bathroom and put some cold water on your face to make sure you are awake. Return to your room and sit in a chair before a lighted candle, a small icon, a Bible, or a small crucifix. Set a timer for fifteen to twenty minutes and then close your eyes and try to be still for the time you have set aside. If you get distracted, return to the stillness by opening your eyes and looking at the symbol you have placed before you, or by repeating a short prayer. When the timer goes off, give thanks to God, bless yourself, and get ready to meet the day.

Book Two

FACING THE QUIET

There is a solitude of space
A solitude of sea
A solitude of death,
but these Society shall be
Compared with that profounder site
That polar privacy
A soul admitted to itself—
Finite infinity.

EMILY DICKINSON, "THERE IS A SOLITUDE OF SPACE"[3]

I once had the opportunity to spend two months in a small desert hermitage. I will not go into the details that led me there, for they are not all that important. And I will not describe the surroundings of my location to any great extent; I will leave that for another time and another place. For the moment, all that is relevant is that I had been longing to go there for quite some time, and I jumped at the first opportunity. Other than that, let it suffice to say that my cabin and its furnishings were simple, the landscape was rugged, and the general atmosphere was conducive to contemplation.

GETTING AWAY

I went to this small, ramshackle cabin in the middle of nowhere because I was fed up with the way my life had been going; everything was moving so fast. I had to juggle a thousand and one things without making a single mistake—and God help me if I did. The weight of the whole world seemed to be on my shoulders. There was no time for second thoughts and no room for uncertainty or doubt. I was on a fast-moving train and I wasn't even sure where I was going. I wanted to get off, but I did not know how; there was no emergency cord to pull or conductor to inform. I was tired, run down, and tense. I was losing interest in my work and getting tense and irritable in the presence of others. I realized that if I did not do something about my situation, I would become controlled—and eventually overwhelmed—by it.

I went to this hermitage to get away from everything, thinking that I would regain my balance by physically removing myself from the stressful situation. Easier said than done, however. Once there, it took me a long time to settle down and find a routine amenable to a solitary existence. Being in a quiet place does not necessarily mean that one will have an experience of quiet, no matter how calm and tranquil things may appear on the surface. Letting go was very difficult. I was so use to "doing" that I had forgotten what it was like to "be." My mind was filled with a whole list of things to do—and it took me quite awhile to resist those subtle and not-so-subtle urges to get them done.

The physical separation from my home and workplace was supposed to have an effect on my internal attitude, but it was hard to get into a frame of mind where I could simply let go. Fortunately, the change in physical location eventually *did* bring about the desired effect, but it took longer than I anticipated. Once certain habits are ingrained in a person's lifestyle, it becomes extremely difficult to change them. In my case, it was not easy to let go and relax because everything I did had been oriented toward some concrete result. It was hard to stop "doing" and to keep myself busy "doing nothing." The more I tried the harder it got.

ACTIVE CONTEMPLATION

The secret, I eventually found, was simply to stop trying so hard. It is not so much a question of what we do, but of the attitude with which we do it. When you think of it, we are *always* doing something; we cannot help it. We are made that way and can do nothing about it. Even the most prayerful contemplatives must occupy themselves with some kind of daily activities. Manual labor, spiritual reading, and liturgical prayer have become the mainstays of the Western monastic tradition—and I doubt it will change. Monks lead busy—even productive—lives. The difference between their attitude toward activity and my attitude, however, is fundamental: I was doing things from the purely utilitarian motive of getting good results, whereas they use their daily activities as a way of drawing themselves closer to God. Their conscious awareness of God, in other words, is intimately tied up with what they do. Their activities are selected, arranged, and scheduled in a way that helps them in their contemplation of the divine.

After a few weeks in my hermitage, I settled into a daily routine that cultivated a contemplative attitude of life. I developed a schedule of my own—one that suited my particular needs. For me, this meant getting up early, eating at regular intervals, and evenly dividing my time in a way that respected each level of my human constitution: physical, emotional, intellectual, spiritual, and social. I was grateful that my hermitage was not far from other cabins, thus making it possible for me to have some genuine human contact at appropriate moments during the day, especially at celebrations of the liturgy and, when desired, mealtimes.

As time went on, I found this flexible routine became more and more a part of my interior rhythm. I was able to do more doing less. I was able to step back, reflect on my activities, and ask myself some profound questions about my reasons for doing what I do. Most importantly, I was able to create more space for God in all that I was doing. Rather than "doing nothing," I was slowly developing the spiritual art of "nothing doing." That is to say, I consciously tried to make room for God in whatever I happened to be doing at the time, even if I happened to be simply wasting time. I was humbled by the thought that I had wasted so little time in the past with the people I love—even God. I hoped the future would be different.

Allowing that little space for God in the particular activities of the day eventually spilled over into the day itself (setting aside an hour of quiet with the Lord), the week (resting on the Sabbath), and the month (making an entire day of retreat). I found that giving this time to the Lord helped me better appreciate the rest of my time. I found myself not only calming down, but growing serene and actually looking forward to whatever quiet time I could set aside during the day.

I was growing quiet, becoming a man of solitude and peaceful calm. I was living not for purposeless activity, but for God. All that I was doing seemed to become incorporated into my contemplation of the divine. It was then that I came to see that contemplation is itself an action—indeed, the highest action a human can ever perform and something that could transform and recapitulate all other activities into a genuine offering of self to God.

Into the Heart

The hermitage became for me an external symbol of my interior conversion of heart. During my time there, my life seeped down within me and made its way into the inner regions of my soul. I internalized my daily routine and, in the process, rebuilt my life from the inside out. I looked within myself and found there a point of stillness that would not be upset by whatever storms raged on the surface. This inner place of refuge, this place of inner quiet and solitude, was able to carry me through the events of the day. I slowly came to see the importance of maintaining this internal sense of quiet at all times. By doing so, I would be able to face whatever turmoil and uncertainty the future might hold.

My time in the hermitage gave me the opportunity to explore the interior regions of my soul. Those inner spaces, I soon found, had a geography all their own. Much of it was sheer wasteland, huge areas of lonely isolation where my inner demons thrived and kept me from coming to terms with my true inner self. In order to enter my interior hermitage, I had to traverse this barren desert of loneliness and overcome my inner thirst for power, possessions, and pleasure. I found, however, that I could not overcome these passions by ignoring them, repressing them, or trying to uproot them from my heart. Rather, I had to journey with them, listen to them, and eventually tame them. Entering the inner hermitage of my heart meant traversing the inner desert of loneliness and isolation. It meant journeying with my inner weaknesses and human frailties, being patient with them so that I could, with the help of God, outgrow them and leave them behind.

I cannot say that I have completed this journey of the heart—at least not yet. I know that I have found a still point within, a place of centering that I call my "inner shelter." I also know that I leave behind the solitude of my heart at times and must struggle to find my way back. I wonder what the future holds for me.

CONCLUSION

My stay in the hermitage taught me the importance of cultivating a contemplative attitude toward life and of recognizing God in all things and in all circumstances. It helped me to let go of time in a way that allowed me *more* time for consciously averting my actions toward God. It also taught me that human actions are important not so much for the material effects they produce, but for what they tell us about the human heart.

Entering the stillness of my heart and learning to rest there has helped me to become patient with myself and others. It has helped me to rest in the present moment and to seek God in all times, all places, and all circumstances. Most importantly, it has shown me how close God is to the human heart and yet how easy it is to forget the gentle, sustaining presence of the Spirit. Life is meant to be lived not on the surface, but at the depths. External appearances, if they are to be true and authentic, must be an expression of what exists in the deepest recesses of the soul. If they are not, we become shallow and insubstantial human beings. If they are, our thoughts, words, and actions become instruments of God's healing love that will transform the inner wastelands of our hearts—and the hearts of others—into a watered garden where we can walk in peaceful fellowship with the divine.

Reflection Questions

1. Have you ever felt that your life was moving too fast and that you had to slow down? Did this feeling come suddenly or did it creep up on you gradually? What was it that made things seem get out of control? Did you do anything about it?

2. Do you find it hard to let go and simply relax? Do you find yourself thinking about your work even in your off time? What practical steps would help you take control of your hectic schedule? Do you think it is really possible to do more by doing less?

3. Have you ever spent an extended time alone? How long was that period of time? an hour or two? an entire day? a week or more? Was it difficult to make this time for your-

self? What did you do during this time? What did you not do? Did you make time for prayer?

4. Do you see a connection between prayer and work, between contemplation and action? Have you ever sensed your work flowing from the deepest part of your being? Do you consider action something complementary or inimical to prayer?

5. Have you ever experimented with prayer forms that might help you more fully integrate being and action? Would you ever consider making an extended private retreat, where you could explore the inner spaces of your heart? What do you think you might find there? Does the phrase "hermitage of the heart" make any sense to you?

EXERCISE

The next time you feel as though things are getting a little out of control, take time out for yourself. Go to a place you enjoy but rarely have time to visit (for example, a park, a nearby chapel, a hiking trail). It doesn't have to be far away, but it should be quiet and you should have time for yourself. For the time you are there—an hour, an afternoon, an entire day—try to get in touch with that quiet point of stillness within you. Place all your worries and concerns in God's hands. Listen to God and let God listen to you. Try to put things in perspective. Give this sacred space within you a name: "hermitage," "shelter," "interior chapel," "inner retreat." When you return to what you were doing, remember that you always carry this point of stillness within you. Remember that God cares for you and that you are never alone.

Book Three
CONTEMPLATIVE READING

In the East a Sage,
beginning his morning praise of the Sun,
saw in the golden titan's place a golden Swan.
In the West an artist looking
at the floating moon watched while,
as if at the touch of his brush,
a floating water-lily bloomed.
As lotus and moon, face-to-face, illumine each other,
light multiplies for the questing eye
to read their bright runes by.

DOROTHY DONNELLY, "METAPHOR'S LAMP"[4]

An old monk retreats to his cell at the end of the evening office. He pulls down his cowl from over his head and loosens his sandals to make himself comfortable. He then sits at his desk, opens the drawer, pulls out his Bible, and turns on his small reading lamp. All this he does without hardly realizing it, as if by rote, so much has the activity become a part of his daily routine. Eying the bookmark that reminds him where he left off the day before, he opens the sacred book and carefully turns to the passage he had set aside for the day. The room is immersed in a pregnant stillness while the monk whispers the words of the sacred reading, just loud enough so that only he can hear his own voice. When he finishes, his eyes move to the beginning of the passage and he reads it again—this time in silence. He repeats the process again and again, stopping at a word or a phrase that touches him or moves him. He waits for the Word to reveal itself to him. He is in no hurry. Time matters little when one is waiting on the Lord. His attention remains fixed not on the words or phrases, but on the inner movements of his heart.

BREAKING THROUGH

Such a reading of the words of Holy Writ takes time to foster and requires much patience. It involves more than just reading the words of the text and trying to understand their literal, surface meaning. Rather, it entails delving beneath their appearances, pondering their inner sense, and breaking through to the deep spiritual meaning within them.

Lectio divina is a masticating, ruminating activity of the soul. Like the prophet Ezekiel, who ate the sacred scroll at God's command (see Ezekiel 2:1–9), readers must chew the words of the text and digest them. They must crack open the words' exterior shell to taste the rich spiritual fruit within. This process, however, cannot be measured or meted out in time; rather, the moment of insight can come after a whole hour of quiet meditation on God's Word or after a few brief moments of intense, awe-inspiring prayer. Breaking open the Word in this way depends more on God than on the reader. It is God who enters our world and gives of himself completely to the point of becoming for us a source of nourishment and hope. This kind of reading is deeply wedded to the mystery of the Incarnation. Such is the meaning of the Word made flesh who made his dwelling among us (see John 1:14).

One does not have to be a monk to reap the benefits of this ancient and venerable approach to the Scriptures, however; people of all walks of life have benefited greatly from this quiet, meditative reading of Scripture. All it takes is the desire to listen attentively to God's Word and to wait for its fertile seed to penetrate the soil of the soul. In this listening and waiting, people have been able to explore many avenues of the spiritual life. And how is this so? Where does one begin? How does one know what to do and what to avoid? The following directives, while by no means exhaustive, can help get interested readers started and point them in the right direction.

1. *Quiet yourself.* Before opening up the Bible, close your eyes and try to recollect yourself. Life can get so hectic at times that it is often difficult to be truly present to the activities you hold most dear. Give yourself time to arrive, to get to where you are. Relax. Try not to think about what you were just doing or what you have to do next. Ask God to help you be present to his Word so that you can listen to it with an open heart. Try to spend a few minutes becoming present to yourself and to God. Only by doing so will you be able to listen from the heart and allow God's Word to penetrate beneath the surface of your experience. This initial moment of quiet is essential for *lectio divina.* Without it you will never be able to appreciate the depth of God's Word and the great relevance it has for your life.

2. *Read the Word.* Once you have gathered yourself into the present moment, open the Scriptures to the passage you wish to meditate on. Do not select a long passage; a couple of sentences or paragraphs will do. Remember, it is not the quantity of words you cover in *lectio divina* that is important, but the depth of what you see. Read the passage through once to make sure you have a sense of its context and general meaning. It may be helpful to have a scriptural commentary at hand to clarify any questions you might have about the literal meaning of the text. Try not to get caught up in the intricacies of the historical-

critical method, however. Although it is an invaluable help to the study of God's Word, it can easily prevent you from encountering and understanding the latent spiritual meanings of the text.

3. *Listen to the Word.* Once you have a good sense of the general meaning of the text, go back to the beginning and read it again—slowly, word by word, phrase by phrase, sentence by sentence. This time, however, don't be concerned about getting all the way through the reading. Rather, be ready to pause—stop, even—when a particular word or phrase catches your attention. Dwell upon the words. Ponder them. Allow them to penetrate your hearing and enter your mind. If it helps, pronounce the words in a soft whisper or out loud. Ask God to help you heed them in the inner sanctions of your soul. Only by listening to the words—by allowing them to speak in their own time and in their own way—will you ever be able to encounter God through them. God is not only the primary author of Scripture; God is its primary interpreter and revealer. The purpose of Scripture is to come into contact with the living Word of God—and that Word comes only to those who listen and wait for its coming.

4. *Ponder the Word.* Ponder what you have listened to, and draw conclusions that are relevant to your life. This means going back over the passage again, looking for particular themes or patterns that speak to your present situation. Reflecting on God's Word means cultivating an openness to the text and waiting with expectant hope for the Spirit of God to touch your heart with the fiery coal of truth. It means going over the text, again and again, until the words enter your soul and become enfleshed. It is then that the words of the text begin to speak to you because they are no longer God's words; rather, they have become your own.

In pondering them and reflecting upon them, you gain a sense of ownership. You can then speak them with conviction because you have listened to them and pondered their depths in your heart. In becoming a part of you, these words become channels of God's grace and draw you closer to the Ground of your being. For this reason, this whole process can best be described as a participation in the action of God's Spirit in your life. By sharing in this process, you come to discover your truest, deepest self.

5. *Act on the Word.* True reflection manifests itself in action. Once you have pondered the text and have made the words your own, something will arise within you that will lead you to express what you have learned. Just as the Word of God has entered your life, given itself to you, nourished you, and enkindled hope in you, now you are called to do the same. Be patient with yourself at this point in the process, however. Allow this word to be born in you. Try not to force it or to get ahead of yourself—or of God's Spirit. There is a close link between who we are and how we act. Allow the being of God, who now inhabits your soul, to manifest itself in your action. To do this you must be especially sensitive to the promptings of the Spirit in your life. Listen to various thoughts, feelings, and intuitions that pass through your mind. Respond to those that conform most closely to the words that have entered your heart and have become enfleshed in your life. Trust them. Act on them. Believe that God is moving you to share the very words that have made such a deep impression on you.

6. *Rejoice in the Word.* God's words do not return void (see Isaiah 55:11). Once you have shared them or put them into action, they swell up again in deep joy that marks the lives of all who are led by the Spirit. At this point in the process be thankful for all that God has done for you.

Rejoice in the Word. Be grateful to God for revealing it to you, for helping you to penetrate its outermost shell, for enabling you to listen to its counsel, and for weaving it into your innermost self. Rejoice in the Word for helping you put it into action that you might be a source of nourishment and hope for others. This aspect of *lectio divina* brings the process around full circle. God glories in the Word as it manifests itself in our lives and in the lives of those with whom we share it. We do the same as we glory in God and in the work God has accomplished in us.

7. *Carry it on. Lectio divina* is a process, a way of reading the Word of God, that has a beginning and an end. That is not to say, however, that this process does not have a residual effect in our everyday lives. On the contrary, its very purpose is to help us experience our daily activities on a deeper level. To do so we need to be able to let go of the process and trust that God's Word abides with us always, even when we are not specifically averting to its presence. It is important for us to let go of the process and to be grateful for what it has given us, but to recognize that life must be lived in the here and now, amidst all of the cares and responsibilities that go along with it. Just as the monk must finally close his Bible and immerse himself in the activities of his monastic routine, so must we be ready and willing to put the Scriptures aside and carry on with our duties and responsibilities in the world. Doing so enables us to live in God's Word without being consciously aware of it from one moment to the next. It allows us to rest in God's Word and trust that God is always leading us, guiding us, and showing us the way.

CONCLUSION

Directives such as those outlined above are meant to *facilitate* your encounter with the living Word of God; they are not to be strictly adhered to in each and every circumstance. In fact, they can be a deterrence in some instances. This holds true especially when they are clung to emphatically—at all costs—despite whatever else the Spirit may be leading you to do.

Lectio divina is not a method; rather, it is an encounter with the living God that takes place in the deepest recesses of the heart, where the divine and human meet, where the Word of God seeks to be born ever new into the world in which we live. This process is not an end in itself, but a way of allowing this birth to take place within us. As such, it asks us to be patient with ourselves and with our God. It asks us to trust that, through it, the relationship we share will not only grow deeper and stronger, but will expand to include an ever-increasing circle of friends.

In the final analysis, *lectio divina* is an invitation to pray. By entering into the Word and allowing the Word to enter into us, we gradually come to see that all of our lives—the conscious and the unconscious, the physical and the intellectual, the social, the emotional and, yes, the spiritual—can be a continuous offering to God. This interpenetration of the divine and the human helps us face the challenges of our daily lives and gives us a deeper insight into the nature of our divine calling. God wishes not only to heal us but also to elevate us, to transform us in such a way that we can share more and more intimately with the One who cherishes us and ever searches for us in the innermost sanctums of the heart.

REFLECTION QUESTIONS

1. Do you find reading a relaxing activity? Does reading put you in a meditative mood and help you settle down? What kind of reading material does this for you? a novel? a book of prayers or meditations? the Scriptures? Have you ever reflected on *how* you read this material and what it is that fosters this contemplative mood in you?

2. Have you ever done a *lectio divina* of the Scriptures? If not, would you consider trying it? What might keep you from trying it? Which part of the process do you think would be most difficult? quieting yourself? the slow meditative reading of the text? listening to the text? pondering the text? acting on it? rejoicing in it? carrying on with it?

3. Are you comfortable with the idea that a text from Scripture can have multiple spiritual meanings? Have you ever come across multiple spiritual meanings in a particular text? If so, how did you come across them? Do you think this experience could be repeated? Do you think it was something you did all alone? Do you think God had anything to do with it?

4. How is meditative reading (*lectio divina*) related to contemplation? Are they identical? Can they be separated? Does one lead to the other—and vice versa? Do they enjoy a circular relationship in any way? In what other ways can the Word of God reveal itself to you? What would your life be like if you never had the opportunity to ponder God's living Word in the Scriptures?

5. Do you think you might be able to deepen your reading of the Scriptures? If so, how? by reading more? by spending more time on a particular text? by asking God to open the

eyes of your heart so that you can understand with greater depth and clarity? Can you think of any practical measures that would open the Scriptures to you even more? Would you be willing to try them?

Exercise

Select a passage of Scripture that you are familiar with and would like to delve into. Before beginning, quiet yourself and ask for God's help. Read the passage through once, and then go back over it more slowly. During this second reading, stop whenever you are struck by something in the text. Repeat the particular word or phrase a few times, and then rest with it. Be still with it. Allow it to enter your bones and sink down into your heart. Try to be attentive to the inner movements of your soul. Ask God to help you understand what is being said to you. Do not worry about finishing the second reading; rather, just listen and wait, listen and wait. After a few minutes, try to formulate, in a single phrase or sentence, God's word to you in general (for example, "Be at peace," "Do not be afraid," or "I am with you"). Try to formulate a more specific phrase or sentence of what God may be asking of you (for example, "Ask forgiveness of this person," "Spend more time in prayer each day," or "Give this person a helping hand"). When you finish, thank God for speaking to you, and ask for help to respond.

Book Four

SEEING BEYOND

Now Say nay
A fig for The seal of fire.
Death hairy-heeled, and the trapped ghost in wood,
We make me mystic as the arm of air,
The two-a-vein, the foreskin, and the cloud.

DYLAN THOMAS, "NOW"[5]

In a quiet corner of her small home, a Russian woman of simple, peasant stock lights a candle before a frameless icon of the Madonna. She bows her head in silence before lifting her gaze to the mysterious presence. There is little need for words in the presence of the Mother of the Word; close friends understand the meaning of life's pregnant silences. There, in the stillness of time, the woman does nothing but rest in the loving gaze of the Mother of her Lord, and the encounter has a gentle, calming effect on her soul.

This quiet, prayerful ritual has been going on for years. Day after day, the woman has found momentary respite from the toilsome chores of life by sharing with her close friend the simple yearnings of her heart. Although her visit lasts only a few short minutes (sometimes less), it has increasingly become one of the defining moments of her day. There before the icon, the woman feels most herself and is utterly at home. Her prayer has slowly transformed her inner awareness of God and has gradually spilled over into everything she does.

Finally, when it is time to go, the woman lets out a sigh from deep within her soul, makes the sign of the cross in her calm Oriental manner, turns toward the kitchen area of her home, lights the fire, and goes about setting the table for her family's evening meal.

WINDOWS TO ETERNITY

The Eastern Churches' long revered tradition of praying before icons offers a concrete way of finding the holy in the ordinary affairs of life. Simple moments such as the one just described remind us of the close bond between sanctity and the routine activities that fill our lives. Such moments also show us how God uses icons as a leaven in our lives to raise our awareness of the presence of the holy in our midst, to mediate to us a contemplative experience in the midst of the most mundane circumstances. As such, icons are welcome reminders of God's deep personal care for our lives and his desire to nourish us throughout our long, harrowing journey to holiness.

Icons are more than just pious pictures, however. The Christian East, for example, regards icons as transparent mysteries, windows through which a person can glimpse the dimension of the eternal in the present moment. An icon "makes present" in a sacramental way the figures it represents: It participates in the world beyond, mediates the life of that world to the onlooker, and serves as an eschatological sign of its final manifestation. Icons are prayer and contemplation turned into art. Supported philosophically by the Neoplatonic notion of participation and rooted theologically by the doctrine of the Incarnation, they lead the beholder out of the dimensions of space and time and into the realm of spirit.

Icons accomplish this amazing feat by mixing two fundamentally opposed means of human expression: symbol and image. While the former evokes the presence of what it represents through a kind of absence, the latter does so through visual reproduction. A wooden cross, for example, is a poignant symbol of Jesus' Passion and death, but differs greatly from a detailed portrayal of his crucified, bloodied corpus. To achieve their effect, icons juxtapose symbols and images to create a sense of the transcendent in our midst. By deliberately combining these opposing forms, they permit neither to reach its natural perfection. The result is a tense balance of countervailing forces that places the icon out of the dimensional boundaries of time and space and brings the beholder to turn his or her gaze to the contemplation of the beyond.

PRAYING THROUGH ICONS

Every person is called to become transparent to the divine life, to rediscover the lost image of God within, to become a living icon of Christ. Prayer is the ordinary means that God has given us to bring about this gradual transformation of our lives and, before an icon, it can assume many shapes. For example, we may sit or stand in front of the icon and simply ponder its meaning; we may use the icon as a focal point for centering prayer or rhythmic breathing; we may simply gaze upon the icon—and allow ourselves to be gazed upon by it in return. Of the various kinds of prayer that are related to icons, three in particular deserve special mention.

1. *The Prayer of Longing:* As a window to eternity, an icon seeks to give us a glimpse into the world beyond; it creates an aesthetic experience that frees it from its relationship to the artist and to those of us who look on it. In effect, the icon takes on a life of its own. It conveys an experience of the transcendent and reminds us that our true home lies in a dimension beyond the confines of time and space. Such a reminder creates a sense of longing in our hearts as we pray. Our spirit, sensing its distant home in the icon's penetrating gaze, knows that it remains a long way away.

This "already-but not-yet" experience can be likened to what the apostle Paul writes about the inward groaning of all who wait for life to come (see Romans 7:23), an inner groaning that extends to all creation (see v. 22) and is in union with the Spirit of God, who expresses our prayer in a way that could never be put into words (see v. 26). Prayer before an icon allows our spirit to resonate with the promptings of God's own Spirit and the yearning of all creation. It provides the human spirit with a concrete point of contact with the transcendent world beyond and enables it to breathe the rarefied air of the Lord's transforming grace.

As we ponder an icon, our inner longing will intensify as we become more and more enamored of God and of divine things. This longing will move in and out of our consciousness in varying degrees and with changing intensities. At times, it may become so intense that we may feel as though God is reaching through the icon and actually pulling us out of the present world and into the next. At such moments, the intervening call to Christian service (*diakonia*) keeps our feet firmly planted on the ground. The day will surely come when one of us must face, alone, that final journey into the beyond. For the time being, however, the Lord usually has other tasks in mind for us.

2. *The Prayer of Presence:* Prayer before an icon can convey a strong sense of God's presence in our personal lives. This is due partly to the Prayer of Longing—which naturally implies a latent presence of the thing longed for—and partly to the heightened spiritual awareness that often accompanies our contemplative gaze. Although they cannot see, persons who are blind possess other sharpened senses that often enable them to detect the near presence of other persons. In a similar way, our heightened spiritual senses sometimes enable us to have a deeper awareness of the divine presence in our heart.

The Prayer of Presence entails a refined sensitivity to the divine accompaniment. It assures us that we are never alone and that God will never abandon one of his children in time of need. The sacramental nature of an icon enables it to mediate this profound awareness of God's presence. It draws us more deeply into the divine mysteries and transforms moments of intense longing into momentary glimpses of Emmanuel, "God with us." It is here where the incarnational foundation of Christian iconography comes to the fore. Prayer should not be thought of as a long-distance conversation with an unseen God who rarely intervenes in the daily activities of our lives. Rather, it is an intimate, living relationship with someone who understands our human limitations, who cares for us dearly, and who promises to be with us on every step of our journey.

This sense of God's presence in our lives often affects the way we view other people. The deeper our awareness becomes, the more clearly are we able to discern the movement in the Spirit in the lives of others. At this point, other people become icons of Christ for us, that is, mediating images for us of God's presence in the world. In turn, as we sense the movement of the Spirit in others, we realize a profound reverence and respect for human life and, by virtue of God's vestigial presence in the world, for all of creation. The Prayer of Presence helps us to relish the wonder of existence that comes to us, moment by moment, from the hand of God, and to stand with awe and a deep sense of gratitude before the ineffable Ground of our existence.

3. *The Prayer of Union.* We are called not just to life, but to life in all its fullness. Our longing for God, and even our deeper awareness of his presence in our lives, tends naturally toward union. Intimacy with God is the work of God, and it can be effected only through our cooperation with the gentle promptings that come through the work of the Spirit.

When praying before an icon, we may receive a brief, ever so fleeting experience of what this union might be like. Imperfect though it may be, prayer before an icon silences our deep inner yearnings and gives us an intense awareness of the divine presence that makes us feel, at least for the moment, completely and utterly at one with the icon. The transparency of the icon to the divine mysteries has so entered into the contours of our spiritual, mental, and bodily makeup that we experience a close harmony with the Spirit throughout our entire being. Such an experience enables us to respond more readily to the promptings of the Spirit in our lives. It gives us a greater appreciation of its gifts and urges us to be ever more receptive to their use in the daily circumstances of our lives.

The Prayer of Union is an intense but passing foretaste of the heavenly banquet. It gives us an experience of the celestial dance that has gone on from all eternity and to which we are invited even now to partake. Here on this earth we are still learning what it means to share in this divine extravaganza. Our first feeble attempts often end in awkward falls and embarrassing missteps. Still, every so often, we seem to get it right. Rather than going off on our own private tangents, we sense, even momentarily, what it means to be completely "in step" with the Lord. We experience the Spirit in our lives so intensely that we seem to know instinctively how to discern and follow its internal movement in our lives.

Three Pertinent Remarks

The following observations now come to the fore:

1. As windows to eternity, icons offer us the opportunity to peer beneath the transitory veneer of life and behold, if only for the shortest part of a moment, the underlying Ground of being toward which all things tend. Praying with and through icons helps us become transparent to

the activity of God's Spirit in our lives. Icons enable us to participate more deeply in the process of our own divinization and propel our gaze forward to that time when all things will be renewed in Christ.

2. No one prays before an icon in exactly the same way. Since everyone's relationship with God is unique in all the world, it follows that the actual manner in which we pray will contain subtle shades of difference. For this reason, it would be a mistake to view the kinds of prayer referred to above as a static framework that must be reflected in exactly the same way in every beholder. On the contrary, we should look for the particular combination of prayer forms that gives our relationship with God its peculiar identifying trait. Although some people may be more prone to one type of prayer than another, the goal here is to find the right blend that suits the personality and individual needs of each believer.

3. Ultimately, it is God who determines the pattern of prayer in our lives and provides us with the correct balance to meet our spiritual needs. God uses icons to mediate those experiences of prayer. Because of their sacramental nature, icons should not be considered ends in themselves, nor thought of solely in terms of their aesthetic value. Icons are only a means to an end; they move us to participate more deeply in the sacramental life of the Church, especially in the Eucharist, which is the icon of Christ par excellence in the world.

Conclusion

"God became man so that man might become divine." This fundamental soteriological principle states well the underlying transformational premise of all iconographic prayer. The icon's juxtaposition of image and symbol points to the union of the human and the divine in Christ; our suspended, contemplative gaze symbolizes our ongoing journey into the mystery of Christ; and the resulting spiritual experience is the presence of God in our midst. God comes to us so that we might be drawn closer to God and eventually become more and more "godlike." Such was the intention of the woman's brief moments of prayer before the icon (noted at the beginning of this reflection). Although the woman might not have been able to express her experience in quite the same way, her constant and persistent prayer before the icon of the Madonna reveals a deep desire to ponder the mystery of Christ in her heart and to respond to the Lord's call in her life in much the same words of her silent, pondering friend: "Let it be done unto me according to your word" (see Luke 1:38).

Mary's response to the angel highlights for us the attitudes of transparency, openness, and cooperation that we are called to foster and make our own during our long and protracted sojourn through life. Like the angel of Luke's Gospel, icons are heavenly messengers who come bearing good news for every pondering heart that takes the time to be still, to listen to the pregnant voices of life's inner silence, and to rest under the healing and elevating warmth of God's penetrating gaze. Through icons, the Spirit shapes us and leads us with the Madonna to the side of Christ and the People of God he came to serve.

REFLECTION QUESTIONS

1. Have you ever prayed before an icon? If so, do you remember which one it was? Do you remember any of the circumstances which led you there? How did you go about praying before an icon? If you have not prayed before an icon, would you be willing to try? Is there a particular icon that you feel drawn to? Would you be willing to pray before that icon in a small chapel or in your room? What is to keep you from doing so?

2. Have you ever been in touch with the inner longing of your heart? What was it like? How would you describe the feeling to a friend? Are there particular times when that longing feels particularly strong? Have you ever felt it while praying before an icon? Did you feel your spirit stirring within you as did so? Do you think the icon had anything to do with the experience? If not, why not?

3. Did you ever sense that the longing within you was turning into a sense of God's presence in your midst? Did you feel that way before an icon? Do you remember the particular image you were praying before? Was it an image of Christ? the Blessed Mother? an angel or a saint? Do you believe that an icon can mediate to you a sense of the person it portrays?

4. Have you ever been lost in prayer, so much so that you lost track of time? What was it like? Were you surprised that this happened? If you have never felt this way, do you believe it could happen to you? Would you feel comfortable asking God to give you a deeper experience of the Spirit? Do you have something to focus on—a passage from Scripture, a lighted candle, an icon—that could help mediate that experience for you?

5. Do you consider prayer before an icon something possible for everyone or for only a select few? Why? Which type of prayer before an icon do you feel most comfortable with? that of urgent longing? of quiet presence? of peaceful union? Which seems the furthest out of reach for you? Can you see yourself praying before an icon in all the ways described above? If not, why not? Can you think of any other helpful ways of turning to God using these special "windows for prayer"?

Exercise

Find an icon of Jesus or the Madonna and Child that you feel particularly drawn to. Hang it on a wall or set it on a table in front of you. Light a candle next to the icon, and turn the lights low. Sitting quietly, keep your eyes fixed on the icon. Do not worry about distractions. When they come, simply call on the name of Jesus and continue your contemplation of the icon. Gaze upon it and allow yourself to be gazed upon by it. Stay with your contemplative gaze for fifteen to twenty minutes. (Use a timer if it necessary.) When your prayer time concludes, stand up, bow before the icon in gratitude, blow out the candle, and give thanks to God for the gift of life.

Book Five

INTERIOR LANDSCAPE

O soul, canst thou not understand
Thou art not left alone,
As a dog to howl and moan
His master's absence? Thou art as a book
Left in a room that He forsook,
But returns to by and by,
A book of His dear choice—
That quiet waiteth for His Hand,
That quiet waiteth for His Eye,
That quiet waiteth for His Voice.

MICHAEL FIELD, "ARIDITY"[6]

Christian monasticism was born in the desert; have you ever wondered why? A recent stay at the Desert House of Prayer on the outskirts of the Saugauro National Park in Cortaro, Arizona, helped me gain some deeper insights into this connection. Of course, the Sonora Desert of the American Southwest is a long way from the desolate regions of Egypt's Upper Nile, where the likes of Antony, Pachomius, and Macarius made the first inroads into what, for the third and fourth centuries C.E., was an innovative and challenging form of Christian discipleship. The differences between the Sonora Desert and the desolate regions of Egypt's Upper Nile, however, do not discount the similarities they share on a spiritual plane. I would like to share with you something of what I have learned.

EXPLORING THE SPIRITUAL LANDSCAPE

I was in Cortaro only a few days when I began to sense the desert landscape resonating within me. What I was experiencing on the outside was somehow a reflection of what was going on inside of me. The feeling, however, is not easy to describe.

The Sonora Desert is hot and dry—but very much alive. The majestic saguaro cactus governs the rugged, mountainous landscape amidst a vast network of shallow desert washes and a varied assortment of plant and animal life. Its low-lying cousins, the barrel, prickly pear and jumping cacti, blanket the plains with their menacing thorns and thistles, making life difficult for even the most determined of bushwhackers. Mountain lions, wolves, coyotes, wild pigs, deer, and rattlesnakes live off the land (and one another) in their never-ending struggle to survive. There, the jackrabbit is ever alert; the roadrunner, in perpetual motion; the hummingbird, in constant search of moisture. In the precarious balance of nature, both predator and prey walk a fine line between life and death. The tables can turn at any moment, leaving vultures to feast on the remains of decaying carcasses.

I had to be exceedingly careful whenever I ventured out from my small desert hermitage in the shadow of the sacred birthing mountain (known today as Safford's Peak), past the ancient Indian markings on the nearby cliffs (known today as Picture Rocks), to explore the uninviting terrain beyond. I always took plenty of water to prevent dehydration; I wore a broad-rimmed hat to ward off the rays of the sun; I waved a walking stick before me to warn any unsuspecting rattlesnakes of my approach; and I marked my trail wherever I went to lower my chances of getting lost. These precautions were reasonable ones, and I took them without a moment's hesitation. Why? Because I wanted to make it back! I grimaced at the thought of something going wrong and my sun-bleached bones being discovered years later by some unsuspecting hiker. "A little too far-fetched," you say? I think not. Experienced desert hikers have told me stories of what could go wrong under the glare of a blazing desert sun—and I thought it wise to heed their warnings.

Even if it was only on a small scale (an Antony or a Pachomius I obviously am not), my time in the desert brought me face to face with the perennial human struggle for survival. Because I felt so small and vulnerable in such a threatening and inhospitable environment, I had to keep my wits about me whenever I wandered off on my own. Every step mattered; there was no one else to fall back on. Just me, myself, and I. What is more, I sensed this struggle was going on not only around me but also within me—and had been for quite some time.

The desert fathers, I believe, went into the desolate wasteland of the Upper Nile to struggle with the elements, yes, but also to wrestle with themselves. In the midst of this intense spiritual conflict, they hoped to get a glimpse of the wandering desert wayfarer who called them there: the God of Abraham, Isaac, and Jacob. They were attracted to the desert because it had nothing to offer them—nothing, that is, but the stark reality of their own vulnerability to the powerful external and internal forces that constantly hounded them. There was also the risk of losing one's mind. An hour's walk in the desert can convince anyone of the fine line between sanctity and madness. In the words of Thomas Merton, "The man who wanders into the desert to be himself must take care that he does not go mad and become the servant of the one who dwells there in a sterile paradise of emptiness and rage."[7] Antony himself could not have put it better. Life in the desert will either make or break you; it will turn you into a saint or a devil; you will either become yourself or lose yourself—and the difference is not always easy to discern.

The Landscape of the Soul

What am I getting at? The desert is a place where the world outside reflects the interior landscape of the soul. It puts us in touch, physically, with our struggle to traverse the vast spiritual wasteland inside of us and to do so with all the precautions of any prudent desert wayfarer. It helps us see our souls writ large in the surrounding terrain, and clarifies for us in the physical realm that which has be going on all along in the spiritual. In this sense, the desert is a symbol of the soul and is understood by our drawing apt analogies with the inner life.

How so? The parallels are sometimes astounding. The water in my canteen, for example, reminded me of my deep inner thirst for God and my need to be constantly close to the life-giving and sustaining spring of God's redemptive love. The protection from the sun afforded by my hat helped me recall my creaturely status before God and the dangers of getting too close too soon to the burning fire of divine love. The walking stick I carried prompted me to remember my need for support along the way and the vigilance I must have for unforeseen dangers at each step of my sojourn through life. The markers I left behind helped me see the importance of memory for this intensely personal journey, where one's next step depends so much on the preceding ones and the way home depends on carefully retracing the trails one has traveled.

The desert fathers learned similar lessons from the inner regions of the Upper Nile. Their distance from human civilization helped them to divest themselves of all unnecessary baggage and to learn the lessons of holy simplicity. The solitary spaces they inhabited put them in touch with their own loneliness and allowed them to experience their inner lives in all that they sensed and experienced. The wild beasts they struggled with enabled them first to see and then to tame the unruly passions that hounded them from all sides of their solitary abodes. The silence of the desert helped them to appreciate the quiet in their souls and to use that calm as a place for the Spirit of God to enter and rest. The desert allowed them to learn about themselves in the midst of their daily struggle for survival. It taught them simplicity and brought them peace; it immersed them in silence and led them to God.

CONCLUSION

The God of the desert calls us out of our smug complacency to explore the vast inner regions of the soul. To do so we must be willing to embark on a protracted spiritual journey that traverses the interior wasteland of discontent and to struggle anew each day to adapt to the harsh extremes of desert existence. The nature of this journey demands that we be alone with ourselves for long stretches of time and at peace with the uncertain outcome of our next step. It also asks us to respect the land through which we are traveling and to be prepared for the dangers and risks awaiting us at every turn.

The desert fathers were drawn to the Upper Nile region because of its close connection with life and death. This desolate wasteland opened their souls and helped them to delve beneath the surface of life so that they could plumb the mysteries of death—and live to tell of it. It beckoned them to lead honest, authentic lives, to be simple and straightforward—to say "yes" when they meant "yes" and "no" when they meant "no" (see 2 Corinthians 1:17)—and to replace needless chatter with silent listening to the One who spoke to them in the depths of their souls.

The desert fathers fled to the interior wasteland of the Upper Nile not to escape life, but to find it. They told their experiences to anyone who would listen and gave birth to a religious movement that has repercussions to this day. In some small way I feel as though my trip to the Desert House of Prayer in Cortaro, Arizona, was in keeping with the spirit of the desert fathers. There the world without revealed to me the interior landscape of my soul in all its immensity, with all its risks and dangers, and with all its beauty. My brief stay showed me that the desert still has many lessons to teach us about the mysterious ways of our always present yet ever elusive God. I left that place much the wiser, having gained a better sense of what the still, small whispering voice within me was saying.

Reflection Questions

1. Have you ever found yourself in a situation where your outer surroundings reflected the state of your soul? If so, describe the situation with as much detail as possible. Has this happened often in your life? Have you ever told anyone about it? If not, why?

2. Have you ever been to the desert? If so, did your time there tell you anything about the nature of your spiritual journey? What did it teach you? If you have never been to the desert, can you think of any moments in your life that would be similar to a "desert experience"? What was the experience like? Did you grow as a result of that experience? Have you ever told anyone about your experience?

3. How would you describe your deepest thirsts? Are they of a physical, emotional, intellectual, social, or spiritual nature? Are they perhaps a combination of a number of these various dimensions of human existence? How do you deal with them? What do you do to relieve them or even quench them? Do you give your thirsts to God in some way? If so, how does God respond?

4. What supports do you need on your spiritual journey? Have you found any structures that have been particularly helpful to you? rituals? types of prayer? spiritual reading? spiritual direction? What role do friends play in your

spiritual journey? Do you talk to any of them about your walk with God? Do you talk to God about your walk in faith?

5. What role has memory played in your spiritual journey? Do you look back at your journey and see where God has led you and may be leading you now? Does marking the trail of your walk in faith help you feel oriented? Does it help you sense where your next step should take you? Can you think of any other ways that the desert experience might reflect something of your inner spiritual journey?

EXERCISE

Imagine you are on a sojourn through the desert. Make sure you know the name of the desert you are in, along with the features of its terrain and its climatic conditions. If you have a difficult time imagining this, try to find a few pictures that will help. As you set out on your walk, make sure that you are well prepared, and make specific note of the various things you have brought along (for example, water, hat, staff). What do you think you will encounter along the way? Are you afraid of getting lost? What hardships do you think are in store for you? Did you forget to mark your trail? How long do you expect to be in the desert? After a few minutes, turn to Matthew 4:1–11 in your Bible and read the account of Jesus' temptation in the desert.

Book Six

DIGGING DEEP

No cars go by
Where dogs are barking at the desert.
Yet it is not twenty years since many lamps
Shed their juices in this one-time town
And stores grew big lights, like oranges and pears.

THOMAS MERTON, "DRY PLACES"[8]

It should not take long for anyone to recognize that deserts, much like cities (albeit for different reasons), are extremely inhospitable to human life. In these places, a person must struggle for survival; it takes stamina and guts to live there. If care is not taken, one may be swallowed up by the land for lack of food, water, and shelter—or, worse yet, driven mad by the unsettling movement of the soul's inner demons. So why would one go there? Why would one face the blazing rays of the sun and its scorching heat? Why would one expose oneself to the endless elemental wear of such barren and isolated wastelands? Why would one put up with such nonstop excruciating pain?

THE DESERT FATHERS

We would have to ask the desert fathers themselves, the likes of Antony and Pachomius, to receive an adequate answer. For now, we will have to settle for the words of Thomas Merton:

> The Desert Fathers believed that the wilderness had been created as supremely valuable in the eyes of God precisely because it had no value to men. The wasteland was the land that could never be wasted by men because it offered them nothing. There was nothing to attract them. There was nothing to exploit....The desert is the logical dwelling place for the man who seeks to be nothing but himself.... But there is another factor that enters in. First, the desert is the country of madness. Second, it is the refuge of the devil, thrown out into the "wilderness of upper Egypt" to "wander in dry places." So the man who wanders into the desert to be himself must take care that he does not go mad and become the servant of the one who dwells there in a sterile paradise of emptiness and rage.[9]

To conquer their temptations and encounter their deepest selves; to be purified by the scorching heat of grace and hear the still, small, rustling sound of God echoing in their souls; to peer across the brink of madness and catch a glimpse of the burning fire of divinity that sustains their every breath: These are the motivations that drove the monks of old into the isolated, deserted places of Sinai and Egypt. The impression it made on their lives and the effect they had on the development of Christian spirituality were so strong that the desert experience itself has become a metaphor for the entire spiritual journey. Down through to centuries Christians have turned, time and time again, to the symbol of the desert to express some of their deepest longings and hopes. We do so even today.

SHIFTING HORIZONS

Times have changed; the world and the culture we live in have changed; we have changed. No longer do throngs of Christian men and women flock to deserted regions to commune with God. With few exceptions, desert monasticism is all but dead—and there is no turning back.

The *symbol* of the desert, however, is another matter; it still has a hold on our collective imagination and brings with it a strange purging effect on our souls. What it stands for has today taken root in the most unexpected of places, somewhere that has become just as barren, just as inhospitable, just as lonely, and just as much a challenge to survival as any barren wasteland inhabited by the great desert fathers of old. It has taken place here, in our very midst, where we live and work and play and try to make ends meet.

We have no need to go out to the desert, of course; the desert has finally found its way to us. It is here, right before our eyes—in the city. It may seem strange to liken the city to the desert, but it shouldn't; many cities of the Western world have degenerated into vast spiritual wastelands. To quote but one contemporary source: "Life in the city today is a wilderness for the masses of men and women who live alone, some worrying about the future, some unconcerned, each unknown to the other."[10] There may be enough food and water to go around, but so many people are dying from loneliness and want of close human ties. They hunger and thirst for an experience of intimacy in their lives, but seem to have forgotten what to do or how to go about it. They feel isolated from one another, fragmented, out of sorts, without purpose or direction. You can see it in the way they carry themselves, in the way they stoop their shoulders, in the way they cast down their heads. You can see it in their eyes. The city has become a desert. It has become the place of struggle and temptation, of purification and wandering, of madness, loneliness and death and, as Merton points out, of despair:

> The desert is the home of despair. And despair, now, is everywhere....Do not think to close it by con-

> senting to it and trying to forget you have consented. ...This, then, is our desert: to live facing despair, but not to consent. To trample it down under hope in the Cross. To wage war against despair unceasingly. That war is our wilderness. If we wage it courageously, we will find Christ at our side. If we cannot face it, we will never find Him.[11]

Over the past fifty years our cities have continued to get larger and larger; more comfortable perhaps, easier to manage in many respects—but they also have become more and more impersonal, much less conducive to authentic human contact. People live in close proximity to one another and yet seem so far away, turning the very spaces they inhabit into that living hell which Dostoevsky so aptly describes as the "suffering of being unable to love."[12]

NUMBING THE PAIN

So what are we to do? How do we get on in this desert of a world in which we find ourselves? What can we do to make sure that we are not overwhelmed by the dangers that lurk in the gloomy shadows of the secular city? Unfortunately, most of us have very low expectations; we just want to get through life without getting burned. We just want to survive. We want to avoid getting stepped on once too often. We want to numb the pain and the loneliness we feel in our hearts and, in the words of T. S. Eliot, to let the world end "not with a bang but a whimper."[13]

Many of us do not want anything more out of life, perhaps because, when all is said and done, we have a hidden suspicion that the world really does not have much more to offer. Deep inside many of us feel like Alberto Knox in Jostein Gaarder's philosophical novel *Sophie's World*: "Life is both sad and solemn. We are let into a wonderful world, we meet one another here, greet each other—and wander together for a brief moment. Then we lose each other and disappear as suddenly and unreasonably as we arrived."[14] Or perhaps the words of F. C. Happold come closer to the mark: "A lonely being, contained in the brief span between birth and death, as a material entity (man) is only an insignificant bundle of atoms in a vast, frightening, impersonal universe, soon to return to dust and be known no more."[15] "To be known no more"—is that not what we are all afraid of?

To numb the pain, we eat, sleep, drink, and work our way through life without ever thinking about what really matters. We simply go about our business, covering up the gnawing pain and loneliness, pretending it does not exist—without ever confronting the ultimate questions of our existence or realizing that everyone else, even those closest to us, is just as lonely. We hold hands and stick together, afraid of being hurt by the cruel outside world, without ever sensing the deeper possibilities of life, death, and human companionship.

Finding God

How do we find God in the secular society we live in? How do we hear that still, small, whispering sound that echoes down the cluttered corridors of the heart and promises to lead us home? How do we begin? How will we be sure that it is the voice of God and not that of the self or, worse yet, the evil one? Let us for a moment return to the symbol of the desert. It has helped us understand the present plight of city living; perhaps it holds for us some unique clues into the kind of wisdom we must choose.

Every analogy limps (sometimes badly), and this image will probably strike different emotional chords in many of us, especially those of us who are sensitive to the growing environmental concerns of this ever-shrinking planet here at the beginning of the third millennium. But do you not find it strange that many of today's wastelands have, because of their rich mineral resources, actually become a source of great material wealth? From the tundra regions of Alaska's Northern Slope to the sand dunes of Saudi Arabia and Kuwait, wells have been dug and great pipelines constructed to bring to the surface and transport for eventual consumption one of the precious commodities of modern living. Where would we be today without oil? Today's cities cannot exist without it; the two go hand in hand. Unfortunately, however, oil just does not drop out of the sky like manna from heaven. It needs to be discovered, mined, pumped to the surface, transported, and processed—all with great care and attentive planning.

In a similar way, when we look at the desert of loneliness that life in secular society has become, we soon recognize that the city's greatest resources are its people, and that we have only recently begun to tap the deep inner riches of the human heart. "Essential things are seen with the heart," says the fox to Saint Exupéry's little prince. The wisdom of the desert, yes, even the desert in the city, proclaims the importance—the absolute necessity—of the inward journey. The desert, one might say, has today become a symbol not only of the city but also of the soul. It tells us that if we want to find God in secular life, we first need to tap the soul's inner resources; we need to explore, mine, and pump to the surface the rich spiritual treasures that lie in the deep interior regions of the heart.

A revered spiritual master once told the story of

> ...a priceless antique bowl that fetched a fortune at a public auction. It had been used by a tramp who ended his days in poverty, quite unaware of the value of the bowl with which he begged for pennies. When a disciple asked the Master what the bowl stood for, the Master said, "Your self!" Asked to elaborate, he said, "All your attention is focused on the penny-knowledge you collect from books and teach-

> ers. You would do better to pay attention to the bowl in which you hold it."[16]

Perhaps, like the poor tramp in the story, we are too close to our greatest treasures to recognize their real worth. Perhaps, like him, we have used our treasures in tasteless and inappropriate ways on account of our ignorance of what they really are. So it is when it comes to things that really count, that is, matters of the heart. So it is also with those particular means that enable us to probe its depths.

CONCLUSION

For some unknown reason many of us, even those of us who are strong believers, who have believed in God for most of our lives, are content with simply getting by. We skim the surface of life and somehow convince ourselves that we are living to the full. We somehow feel that there really is not much more to learn, nothing more to explore, nothing that we can offer or receive from life. But there we are wrong, so very, very wrong.

Jesus once retreated to the desert (see Mark 1:12–13), and his Spirit now beckons us to do the same. If we want to do more than merely survive in the desert of modern city life, we need to go beneath the surface of things and be willing to explore the inner recesses of our hearts. We need to bring to the surface the rich spiritual strength that God imparts to our souls.

Life in the desert is never easy; it takes hard work, patience, and the guts to make serious decisions about the way we live. We must learn to respect the desert of city life, befriend it, learn the secrets of the land, and make the best of what it offers. We need to know ourselves better; otherwise, we may never sense the presence of God within us or recognize him in the face of the stranger. We need to choose our companions wisely, for our lives may one day depend on them. We need to choose our wisdom wisely; otherwise we may never become wise in the eyes of God. Most of all we need to trust in God, for God alone can lead us through the spiritual wasteland of loneliness that is our modern secular society. He *said* he would do it; he *promises* to do it; he *will* do it. *Without* him we can do nothing; *with* him all things are possible. *With* him we can plant and cultivate a verdant garden in the surrounding spiritual wasteland of secular life, and there will be a great harvest—enough to feed our own and many other hungry and thirsty hearts.

REFLECTION QUESTIONS

1. Do you live in a city? If so, can you see similarities between living in a city and the desert experience? Can you see dissimilarities? If you do not live in a city, do you think you would have a difficult time adapting to city dwelling? What would be the greatest benefit for you if you lived in a city? What would be the greatest disadvantage for you? How would living in a city affect your spiritual journey? Would it have a positive or a negative effect on you?

2. Do you know your neighbors? How many doors or houses away are they? Are there neighbors within a five-minute walk that you don't know well enough to say "hello" to? Would you recognize that they were your neighbors if you passed them on the street? How do you deal with the increasing sense of anonymity existing in city, suburban and, to some degree, rural life? What practical steps can you take to ameliorate the situation?

3. Do you think you are lonelier than most people? If so, why? Have you ever thought about why or how you get lonely? Can you put your finger on any particular circumstance that would make you prone to feeling lonely? Have you thought about positive steps that might help you alle-

viate your loneliness? If so, what are they? Have you tried them? If not, what keeps you from doing so?

4. Have you ever felt as though you were living only on the surface of life? How would you describe this feeling? uneasy? depressing? uncertain? human? What efforts have you made to tap into the rich resources below? What does "mining the riches of the human heart" mean to you in the practical circumstances of your life? Can you think of any concrete steps you can take to have a deeper experience of God in the midst of the ordinary events of the day? If not, is there anyone who might be able to help you?

5. Do you belong to a local faith community? How would you describe that community? How many members belong to that community? What are the positive and negative elements of belonging to this faith community? Does the community reinforce the typical "herd mentality" that is increasingly found in our cities, or does it enable you to see more clearly, to think for yourself, and to reach for goals that you would otherwise be helpless to achieve? In what ways does participation in community ease the trials of the desert experience in contemporary city living?

Exercise

Imagine you are in a big city thousands of miles from the small, rural town where you grew up. You are now living in a tall high-rise and you don't know your neighbors. You feel lonely, depressed, out of touch, disconnected. You don't know how you ended up in this place, and you feel strangely trapped by your job commitments—a job you don't even like. You refuse to feel sorry for yourself, however, and decide to do something about your situation. What would you do to survive in this desert wasteland? What steps would you take to improve your situation?

Book Seven

THE PRAYER OF JESUS

There is a bolder way,
There is a wilder enterprise than this,
All-human iteration day by day.
Courage, mankind! Restore Him what is His.

ALICE MEYNELL, "THE LORD'S PRAYER"[17]

The parish community is gathered for Sunday Mass. The priest at the altar, having just finished the eucharistic prayer, looks out into the congregation, raises his arms to heaven, and invites the people to join him in praying to the Father as Jesus did. Some people in the community raise their arms, some join hands, some simply bow their heads. They pray in unison and in measured cadence as the words of the Our Father roll from their lips. Although many do not seem to realize what they are saying, some are reflective and some pray the words straight from the heart.

All those gathered in this community are disciples, like those who went before them, asking their Lord to teach them how to pray. By using the very words Jesus taught, they hope to be graced with something of Jesus' interior state of heart and mind. Deep in their hearts, below their conscious selves, their spirits yearn to be in constant touch with their Lord.

To Pray As Jesus Prayed

Have you ever wondered why the disciples asked Jesus to teach them how to pray (see Luke 11:1)? Did they not know how to pray? Were they not aware of their own Jewish traditions? Did they not pray to Yahweh in the way prescribed by Jewish law? What was it that they sensed in Jesus that made them want to pray the way he prayed? What did Jesus have that they did not have?

Obviously, the disciples sensed something. They saw in their Master someone who enjoyed a close, intimate relationship with God, something they found lacking in their own lives. Jesus' response was to open to them his own life of prayer, to show them how he himself prayed to the Father. And he did this not so much with words but with his whole bearing and manner of expression: "When you pray, say: Father, hallowed be thy name. Thy kingdom come. Give us each day our daily bread; and forgive us our sins, for we ourselves forgive every one who is indebted to us; and lead us not into temptation" (Luke 11:2–4).

As inspiring and beautiful as these words are, however, one must take care not to lose sight of Jesus' reasons for saying them. The words are *his* prayer, the Lord's prayer. He did not recite them to instruct his disciples in the methods of oral composition. Nor was he conducting a religion class in which he expected his followers to recall perfectly everything he said. (There are, in fact, two versions of the Lord's Prayer: Matthew 6:9–13 and Luke 11:2–4.) Rather, Jesus was simply trying to show his friends how to converse with God and, to do this, he had to manifest the deepest longings of his own heart. The words of the Our Father were the means he chose to accomplish this one, all-important task.

Jesus poured himself into these words. He prayed them with all his heart, mind, soul, and strength to show his disciples how they, too, must offer all of themselves to God when they pray. The words were secondary to the attitudes of mind and heart that informed them. They were the verbal expression of Jesus' deep communion with the Father, an experience he wanted to share with his closest disciples. Jesus wanted to tell his disciples that authentic prayer involves the entire self. He wanted to give them more than just words to guide them in their prayer; he wanted to teach them *by showing them how*, by praying to his Father right before their eyes. It would be up to them to follow his example by allowing each petition to resonate in the deepest part of their souls.

Over the centuries the Lord's Prayer has become one of the most popular forms of Christian prayer. It is a truly ecumenical prayer, one that easily flows from the lips of all believers regardless of their denominational affiliation. It has a home in both the liturgy and in popular devotions. It crosses social barriers and finds a place in the homes of rich and poor alike. Few prayers have such a broad, universal appeal; few have the potential to draw people together and to create among them a strong, common bond. At the same time, few prayers have failed so miserably in adhering to the original intentions of its author!

"Familiarity breeds contempt," as the saying goes, and even prayers of divine origin can fall victim to the sayings of worldly sages. The Lord's Prayer is no exception. It has been recited so often and so mechanically that it sometimes resembles more a superstitious incantation of the gods than a humble prayer from the heart. Many simply take it for granted, believing that a mere recitation of the words somehow fulfills the basic requirements of authentic Christian prayer. Others have learned to detach themselves from the words, so much so that their minds and hearts are thousands of miles away as their lips sound the words given them by their Lord. Still others simply no longer make the effort; the words of the prayer no longer carry any meaning for them.

In the Lord's Prayer, Jesus gave his disciples a special

glimpse into his intimate life with the Father. It was a moment that words themselves could not contain, not even words as beautiful as those in this prayer. It was a moment of insight, a moment when the disciples came to see their call to an intimate relationship with the Father. It was an experience they would never forget, one they would share time and time again with those placed in their care.

Christians today know the words of the Lord's Prayer but can easily lose touch with the spirit that inspired them. We recite the prayer often, and even with devotion, but can easily overlook the unique invitation it offers. To prevent this from happening, we need to delve beneath the words and try to get in touch with the experience the Lord was trying to convey. Now more than ever we need to put ourselves in the place of Jesus' closest disciples and voice once more the probing question that inspired their Master to do what he did. Now it is *our* turn. With the words he gave us in our hearts and on our lips, we must turn to him and humbly ask, "Lord, teach us to pray." Once we do this, the words of the Lord's Prayer will present themselves in an entirely different light. Like Jesus' disciples, we will see for ourselves the rich, intimate life we can have with the Father—and the Father with us.

The Jesus Prayer

One of the best ways of getting in touch with Jesus' attitude of mind and heart is through the Jesus Prayer: "Lord Jesus Christ, have mercy on me!" These seven simple words, deeply rooted in the traditions of the Eastern church fathers, were made famous by such religious classics as *The Philokalia* and *The Way of the Pilgrim* and represent an attempt to respond to the apostle Paul's injunction in 1 Thessalonians 5:17 "to pray without ceasing." The beauty of this prayer is that it addresses every level of human existence and can thus be prayed at various times and in different ways throughout the day. It can be prayed by anyone, regardless of his or her facility with the ways of prayer; beginner and master alike can benefit from the peace and calm imparted by the simple repetition of these words.

I offer the following suggestions for praying the Jesus Prayer:

1. Memorize the Jesus Prayer and repeat it out loud and often, with conscious deliberation; the volume does not really matter. You can say the words in a clear, conversational style, in a low whisper, or with no sound whatsoever—just a mere movement of the lips as the words flow silently from your breath into the surrounding air. The important thing is to move the lips while praying so that the words are given clear physical expression. In this way, the prayer addresses the bodily dimension of who you are and enables you to offer it up to God in a song of praise and thanksgiving. Those with more experience in praying the prayer find that the words eventually become in sync with their breathing and the beating of their hearts. The more they pray it, the easier it is for them to offer this all-important bodily dimension of their lives to God in prayer.

2. Allow your emotions to enter into the Jesus Prayer by being willing to permit your feelings to come through the words as they are repeated out loud or uttered silently in some quiet corner of your heart. Actually, you need not confine yourself to the words of the Jesus Prayer; any short phrase or expression that can generate emotion will do (for example, "Lord Jesus, I love you" or "Lord Jesus, help me"). Laying bare your emotions to God is the primary purpose of such short fervent prayers. The words of the Jesus Prayer can (and should) be adapted in a similar fashion because the emotions, too, form an essential dimension of human existence. If our emotions are not raised

to God in prayer, something will be lacking in the way we relate to God.

3. Allow the prayer to enter and reverberate throughout your mind. Focus on the words and mull over them so that you can penetrate and understand the meaning they are intended to convey. Consider the words "Lord Jesus," for example, and ask yourself if you truly relate to Jesus in the way the words imply—as Lord, as Savior. Do the same with the word "mercy" and then consider reading and reflecting on a related passage from Scripture. You might want to sit still, repeat the words of the prayer, and try to imagine the Lord Jesus extending a merciful hand to you or someone you know. Gradually, the prayer becomes more and more meaningful and the words themselves, "Lord Jesus, have mercy on me," begin to penetrate the deeper recesses of your mind. At this point, the Jesus Prayer becomes a veritable form of Christian "meditation."

4. Pray the Jesus Prayer with others. Community prayer addresses the social dimension of human existence and reminds us of how much we depend on one another. As the words of the Jesus Prayer are repeated for a given period of time (for example, five or ten minutes) in a gentle rhythm, a quiet bond forms among those who are praying. Such prayer celebrates the unity of the human spirit in the midst of the diversity of gifts and talents that God has poured into his Body. It brings to the fore the vast web of relationships that touches every human life and opens up to God in a communal but distinctly contemplative manner. In praying with others in this fashion, you come to realize that you are related to and depend upon others on the deepest levels of human existence. The bond you share with others touches the core of the human heart and communes with God's Spirit as a vibrant, believing community.

5. Finally, pray the Jesus Prayer with your spirit. Sit still and allow the peaceful repetition of the words, however you care to say them, to sink into the quiet of your heart where they can touch the deepest part of your center. Allow the words to shape the silent yearning within yourself and to give voice to the unutterable groanings of your heart. It is then that the Jesus Prayer actually becomes one with the prayer of your heart. It is then that the words fade into the background and your spirit communes with the Spirit of God in a deep, intimate embrace of love. Here, silence reigns and words are no longer necessary. God's Spirit reaches out and touches your spirit—and you reciprocate. You listens to each other and seek the other's well-being. Silence grows within and gives birth to the Word in the life-giving womb of the heart.

CONCLUSION

The Jesus Prayer can be prayed in a way that addresses each of the five dimensions of human existence: physical, emotional, mental, social, and spiritual. That is not to say, however, that each person will use the prayer to address these dimensions in exactly the same way. While all these dimensions are important and need to be addressed, each individual normally leans toward one (or several). One person may feel comfortable praying the Jesus Prayer aloud; another may prefer to use the Jesus Prayer as a short, ejaculatory prayer; another may prefer to meditate on its words; another may want to pray the prayer with others; another may prefer to hold the prayer in silence. These differences in emphasis are important and should be encouraged, since they are precisely what makes each individual's relationship to God so unique. At the same time, our preferences toward one dimension should not lead us to overlook (or even neglect) the other ways in which the Jesus Prayer can be prayed. The goal in all this is to find the right balance that allows the five dimensions of human existence to be adequately expressed through the prayer. This personal rhythm will deepen our own self-understanding and draw us closer to the divine mystery in whose image we have been made (see Genesis 1:27).

Reflection Questions

1. What was Jesus trying to teach his disciples when they asked him how to pray? Do you think he was trying to teach merely the *words* of the Lord's Prayer, or was he trying to teach something more? Do the words really matter? How do you pray the Lord's Prayer? What can you do to pray the Lord's Prayer so that it will be more in keeping with Jesus' original intention of fostering an intimate relationship with God?

2. What did the apostle Paul mean when he exhorted the Thessalonians "to pray without ceasing" (1 Thessalonians 5:17)? What relevance might this statement have to your own prayer life? How might it affect your life? Would your life be any different on the surface? Would it be any different within? Do you think anyone would notice a difference?

3. Have you ever prayed the Jesus Prayer? If not, would you be willing to try it? If you have prayed the Jesus Prayer, did it help you understand what Paul meant when he said, "pray without ceasing"? Which way of praying the Jesus Prayer proved most beneficial to you? Is there one particular way of prayer that you tend to neglect?

4. Can you see yourself praying the Jesus Prayer on all five of the dimensions of human existence outlined above: physical, emotional, intellectual, social, and spiritual? How

would you go about finding the rhythm of praying this prayer that would be most suitable to you? Do you think you have to be conscious of this rhythm to be at genuine prayer? Do you think you have to be conscious of the words themselves to be praying the prayer?

5. Like the disciples, have you ever asked Jesus to teach you how to pray? Have you ever asked him to teach you how to "pray without ceasing"? If so, what kind of response did you get? Have you ever thought that the Spirit of God might be communing with your human spirit? Have you ever thought that prayer is as much a work of God in your life as it is a work of your own—perhaps more? If you have never asked Jesus to teach you how to pray, what is to keep you from doing so now? Do you think it is too late to ask? Do you think that God is not interested or will refuse to answer your heartfelt prayer?

EXERCISE

Out loud, in a soft whisper, or in silence, pray the Our Father slowly and meditatively, pausing between each phrase. Listen to the words and make sure you understand what you are praying. After you finish, close your eyes and recite the Jesus Prayer: "Lord Jesus, have mercy on me. Lord Jesus, have mercy on me." Continue for several minutes and, as you pray, be conscious of your breathing; try to align your words within its inner rhythm. Then recite the Our Father again, this time aloud and at a normal pace. Repeat the whole process a second time.

Book Eight

REFRESHING WATERS

I dreamed that, as I wandered by the way,
Bare Winter suddenly was changed to Spring,
And gentle odours led my steps astray,
Mixed with a sound of water's murmuring
Along a shelving bank of turf,
which lay Under a copse,
and hardly dared to fling
Its green arms round the bosom of the stream,
But kissed it and then fled,
as thou mightst in dream.

PERCY BYSSHE SHELLEY, "THE QUESTION"[18]

I once had the opportunity to visit the refreshing blue waters of Vaucluse in the southern French province of Provence. Tucked away in the steep, cascading foothills of Mont Ventoux, this deep, motionless pool feeds a small bubbling stream that runs a long and winding course to one of the many tributaries of the Rhône and eventually out to the Mediterranean Sea. Known for its perfect stillness at the surface and its unfathomable depths below, Vaucluse captures the imagination of the curious and has a strange, calming effect on the soul. For centuries pilgrims have made their way to this small quiet spot to ponder its still, descending waters. They have done so, in part, to see if their gaze could penetrate the pool's surface water to its distant bottom; in part, yearning for the tranquillity and depth they long for but do not possess; in part, to see the faces of their souls reflected in the clear blue presence before them. The waters of this quiet mountain pool invite onlookers to delve beneath the surface of things to ponder the depths of life's silent, interior flow. So it was in my own case and, I would imagine, in the lives of many others.

A SYMBOL OF PRAYER

It took me the better part of an hour to follow the small mountain spring to its source. Along the way I stopped to witness the flowing white water as it navigated the various rocks, logs, and other untimely obstacles that got in its way. I marveled at the motion and wondered what I would find at its origin. Could the pool really be as still and deep as the stories claimed it to be? How could water so still and so deep produce a rushing stream like the one before my eyes?

Picking up my pace, the narrow path gradually dwindled in size as it brought me closer and closer to my goal. Before I knew it, the beautiful pool was right before me, tucked away just as I had imagined. It was nearly hidden from view by the steep chalky cliffs that towered above it, providing it a majestic rocky background. The water in the pool was calmer than I thought it would be, wrapped in a stillness that suggested some deep, subterranean flow in the bowels of the mountain beside me.

"Still water runs deep," as the saying goes. The waters of Vaucluse confirm, in a concrete, natural way, the truth of this popular proverbial expression. As I stood by the side of the pool gazing into the still, silent water, I felt myself captivated by its mysterious downward pull. Staring into it, I gradually became immersed in its stillness and soon sensed—floating across the periphery of my consciousness—a deep (and thoroughly unexpected) insight into the ongoing movement of my life. *Like the rushing mountain stream that has its source in a deep watery stillness, my own actions must flow from the silent depths of my soul's intimate union with God. If they do not, they will be cut off from their source and will eventually run dry. If I allow this to happen, I will be doing irremediable harm to myself and unnecessary damage to others. Such an occurrence would be a terrible waste of life and manifest a great lack of reverence for God, my neighbor, and myself.* The conclusion I came to was crystal clear and, to my mind, irrefutable: *I must never allow the flowing stream of life to run dry in me. If I do not nurture the spiritual side of my existence, dire consequences will follow. Prayer is one of the most fruitful and life-giving activities I can engage in; everything in my life must flow from it.*

I had been at the pool for only a brief while and already I was reaping spiritual benefits that would stay with me the rest of my life. I could not help but wonder how many others had been similarly aided by pondering this small, quiet pool of water in the south of France. Since much of the fountain's past is shrouded in legend and myth, there is no way of telling for sure. Even these legends and myths, however, can tell us something about the role the still waters have played in the lives of those who have felt its powerful allure.

Of the many tales inspired by this mysterious pool and preserved in the local lore of the region, one in particular deserves special mention. Like my own experience at the pool, it finds deep religious symbolism in the water's life-giving flow. Unlike my experience, however, it examines the dark side of human existence and tells us how to lessen its damaging influence in our lives.

Taming the Beast

This legend dates back to the sixth century A.D. and tells of a monster that once lived in a nearby cavern that guarded access to the pool's calm, silent water. This horrible beast terrorized the inhabitants of the region and left a path of death and destruction wherever it went. Years of living in terror had taken its toll on the people and finally brought them to their knees. They turned instinctively to their saintly bishop, Véran, a man known far and wide for his wise decisions and deep, peaceful spirit.

After summoning the villagers to church, Véran calmed their fears with words of Scripture, fortified them with the sacred bread, and then led them out to confront the beast who blocked all access to their precious pool. When they reached the mouth of the cave, Véran commanded the beast to come out from hiding and face the judgment and just punishment of God.

What happened next surprised everyone present, perhaps even the old saintly bishop himself! The monster crawled out of its cave, its head low and its tail between its legs, and made its way to the feet of the holy man. As the monster laid its head on the ground as a sign of complete and total submission, the bishop scolded the beast for the evil it had done, sprinkled it with holy water, and warned it never to incite such fears again. To be sure that the beast would nevermore terrorize the inhabitants of the village, the bishop put an iron chain around its neck and fastened the end of the chain to the wall of the cave, thus leaving the monster little room for carrying out further wrongdoing. Overcome with joy at the sight of this incredible turn of events, the people of the village praised the name of the Lord, cheered their bishop for the miracle he had performed, and made their way to the pool, where they drank from its cool, refreshing water for the first time in many years.

Today, most people would react to this charming tale with a smile (bordering on a smirk) that would betray either disbelief in something like this actually happening, or nostalgia for an earlier, less sophisticated age that naively accepted the power of divine intervention in the ordinary affairs of life. For our purposes, although this legend has little (if any) basis in history, it certainly has a great deal to tell us about the spiritual dimension of our lives.

What lesson could we possibly wean from such a simple tale? Its meaning is evident to anyone who takes the time to delve beneath its surface imagery and ponder its hidden message. To drink from the waters of a bottomless spring stands for the journey of self-knowledge and our willingness to explore the inner depths of the soul. The hideous monster that guards the pool and creates havoc throughout the region represents everything within us that prevents us from exploring those deep interior regions (that is, inordinate passions, destructive habits, deadly vices). The fact that this monster lives in a deep cavernous cave means that we may be unconscious of some of these destructive tendencies in our lives. The terror and devastation caused by the monster point to the sad external effects that these dangerous leanings have in our lives. The holy bishop represents the voice of wisdom that is steeped in prayer and present in Christ's Church. The procession to the cave represents our firm resolve to face our inner demons, whatever the consequences. The calling forth of the beast and its miraculous taming symbolize the power of God to exorcise the soul's inner demons and to effect a permanent change in our lives.

When viewed in this light, the legend tells the story of the intense inner drama of the soul's conversion. Its popularity comes precisely from the way it calms the human psyche with powerful religious symbols that go beyond the threshold of the visible world and mediate the power of the transcendent in our midst. Pregnant with deep religious meaning, the tale speaks to the heart and offers hope to those cut off from the deep spiritual source that promises to nourish them and make them whole.

Conclusion

For centuries, the waters of Vaucluse have sparked the religious imagination of all who have come to ponder its clear, tranquil surface and stare into its unfathomable depths. Besides the wonder it inspires by its own natural beauty, it also reminds us of the centrality of prayer in our lives and the great urgency incumbent upon all of us to calm the raging passions of life's inner demons. The quiet pool does not force these or any other conclusions on anyone, but merely elicits them from the hearts of those who take the time to sit by its side, ponder its deep, quiet strength, and listen to one or more of the imaginative tales that have accompanied it on its journey through the ages. Those who take the trouble to do so will never regret it. Such is the spell that this quiet pool casts over those fortunate enough to follow its fast rushing waters to their source.

REFLECTION QUESTIONS

1. Have you ever felt the need to delve beneath the surface of things and ponder the depths of life's silent, interior flow, much like the pilgrims stare into the still waters of Vaucluse? If so, what were the circumstances that brought this about? Was it an experience of nature? an encounter with another person? something you read? Did you do anything about it? If not, why?

2. How do the forces of darkness manifest themselves in your life? Do you act out of them? Are you fully conscious of them? Do you listen to them? Do you follow them? Do they control you? If so, in what ways? How do you deal with them? How can you silence them? heal them?

3. Do these inner demons wreak havoc in your external work as well as in your interior world? Do they have an effect on your relationships with your family and friends? Do they have an effect on your relationship with your community? on your relationship with God? How can these relationships be healed?

4. Where do the voices of wisdom in your life come from? from within your heart? from the voices of those who care for you? from the Scriptures? from the sacraments of the Church? from those given positions of authority? Can you hear these voices? How do you react to them? Are they always in concert? Do they sometimes give you mixed signals? In what ways do they confront your inner demons? In what ways do they exorcise your inner demons?

5. Do you feel the need for cleansing and healing in your life? In what areas? How do you go about seeking cleansing and healing? Is this need deeply rooted in your heart? Do you feel capable of being healed? Have you ever laid bare these areas of your life to God? Do you believe that God can exorcise your inner demons and heal you of whatever havoc they have wreaked in your life? Do you believe that God can transform you and lead you along the way of conversion?

EXERCISE

Find a still pool of water and stare into its motionless depths. If necessary, improvise; a large bowl of water will do. Try to see your reflection in the water. Can you see yourself? Do you recognize your own facial features? Reach down and touch your image on the surface of the water. Watch the water as its ripples distort your face and eventually find their way back to stillness. Now close your eyes, and imagine that the pool of water is within you. Look down into its motionless depths and try to see your reflection. Try to stir the waters with your hand. Do you see any ripples? any distortions? Watch the pool within as it makes its way back to stillness. Now turn to Psalm 23:1–4, and read: "The Lord is my shepherd; I shall not want. In verdant pastures he gives me repose; Beside restful waters he leads me; he refreshes my soul."

Book Nine

MOUNTAIN HEIGHTS

Beautiful must be the mountains whence ye come,
And bright in the fruitful valleys the streams,
wherefrom Ye learn your song:
Where are those starry woods?
O might I wander there,
Among the flowers, which in that heavenly air
Bloom the year long!

ROBERT BRIDGES, "NIGHTINGALES"[19]

At least once a year (sometimes more), usually during the summer months when I am on vacation and have some time to myself, I climb a mountain. Usually, it is not a particularly tall mountain—but it isn't unusually small either. It is "manageable," one clearly marked, with a gradual, winding ascent that someone like myself can manage without too much trouble and without fear of falling or, worse yet, getting lost.

I have been climbing mountains for as long as I can remember, sometimes with friends, sometimes by myself. I enjoy the quiet of the woods, the sound of rushing mountain streams, the spectacular views, the wildlife, the closeness to the earth. It never really matters to me which mountain I climb, although I have my favorites. And I have made it a point not to travel long distances to find one. New York and New England provide me with more mountains than I know what to do with and will keep me well occupied (and content) for many summers to come.

A Memorable Climb

I remember one particular summer day a couple of years ago when I had my sights on the summit of Slide Mountain, the tallest of New York's Catskills at 4,204 feet. Slide Mountain is located deep in the woods of Shandaken Township not far from Phoenicia off Route 28.

The ascent was much easier for me than it was for John Burroughs, the famous American woodsman and naturalist who blazed the trail late in the nineteenth century and found it the most inaccessible of the Catskills, shielded as it was by so many other lofty, wooded peaks. The trail did have its share of steep upward slopes and obstacles, however, and proved to be one of the more difficult climbs I have attempted.

The Wittenberg-Cornell Slide Trail, as it is now called, is 8.9 miles long. It begins at Woodland Valley, is marked in red and, although known as a trail for experienced hikers, is well traveled and easy to follow. Although I was alone on this particular day, I greeted a few other hardy hikers and backpackers along the way. From them I learned that an approach from Big Indian Pass along Route 47, just past Winnisock Lake, offered an easier route to the summit and would, in fact, cut my hiking time in half, perhaps more. I tucked this piece of information away for another day; after all, who knows when and with whom I would return? For the moment, I was resolved to stick by my chosen course, regardless of the time it would take. I was not in any hurry and, besides, half the fun is in getting there, at least so I thought. The approach I had chosen was difficult because it traversed the rugged landslide that gave the mountain its venerable name. Although I took my time during the ascent, I have to admit that the heat of the day and the difficulty of the climb made me eager to reach the summit.

After a grueling six-hour hike under the burning midsummer sun, I reached the top and knew immediately that the trip was worth the effort; I was utterly speechless at what I saw. There, in clear view, the entire Catskill range, all seventy peaks, stretched out before me with Cornell and Wittenberg the nearest in view and the great Ashokan Reservoir just beyond them. There was the Taconics and Hudson Highlands to the west, and the rolling Shawangunks to the south. Referring to my map, I even thought I could make out the Green Mountains of Vermont and the Berkshires of Massachusetts off to the north and the west. What a sight! I thanked God for the clear sky and the gentle breeze. The view was simply spectacular.

As I took in the beauty of the moment, my eyes glanced down to one of the granite boulders at my feet, where I noticed a worn metal plaque giving Burroughs's own description of what he had seen. It read: "Here the works of man dwindle." I could not have found a more accurate phrase to express what I was feeling. Those words confirmed for me what I had always sensed about the act of climbing a mountain: There is something fundamentally religious in it. At the top, one always hopes to catch a glimpse of the transcendent—that, at least, is how it was with me. I certainly realized what I had hoped for. I felt inwardly renewed and spiritually refreshed—and I would not soon forget it.

THE HUMAN JOURNEY

By now, my love for climbing mountains should be obvious. When I am climbing, I feel as though I am fulfilling part of the task for which God created me. I was made to climb, to transcend the boundaries of my life, to bring out my greatest potential, to realize my deepest hopes. Every mountain ascent encapsulates for me the various stages of my journey through life and helps me experience them as an ordered, harmonious whole. Each stage of the climb expresses in a physical way what I am going through in every other dimension of my life. Each mountain ascent becomes for me a ritual enactment that helps me recognize and deal with many of the tensions I otherwise would not openly avert to. Here is a simple listing of what I do. The actions speak for themselves—and on many levels.

1. *The preparation stage:* I start by locating the mountain on the map and charting a suitable trail that will take me to the summit. I also keep an eye on the weather so that I can plan my climb for a day when the chances of having a clear view at the top are good. I also make sure that I have enough food and water to last me for the day, that I am wearing the proper clothing, and that my staff and hiking boots are in descent condition. I pack my gear in a small knapsack and make sure to include a small first-aid kit to care for any cuts or blisters I may get along the way. In addition to all of this, I make sure that my car is ready to take on whatever mountain roads I may ask it to climb. I then drive to the base of the mountain and begin my climb.

2. *The ascent stage:* At this point, I make sure that I am on the right trail by keeping an eye out for trail markers. I begin with a slow steady pace and take in the scenery up ahead and on either side of me. I walk with anticipation for what I will find at the top, never quite sure who or what I will find or what I will see. As I make my way up the trail, I often find myself day dreaming, singing songs, joking with those I am with or, if I am alone, talking to myself. I act differently on the way up from the way I act on the way down. On the way up, I am usually curious and playful. I take frequent breaks and am in no great rush. Life is full of adventure, and everything seems possible.

3. *The resting stage:* When I finally reach the top, I usually stand for a while to stretch out my arms, take in the sight, and survey my surroundings. I then find a nice place to sit and rest. I usually don't spend a great deal of time on the top, just enough time to rest, eat my lunch, say a prayer, and enjoy the view; an hour or so normally does the trick. This is the quickest and usually the sweetest part of the day. I rest and relax at the end of a long morning of climbing before I pack up my things and retrace my steps down the mountain.

4. *The descent stage:* I usually say very little on my way down, partly out of fatigue and partly from a desire to process all that I experienced on the way up, especially at the summit. I think back over the events of the day and begin to think of what I need to do once I get home, thus beginning reentry into my workaday world. The descent gives me time to take my leave of the mountain. I walk as quickly as possible but try to maintain a meditative mood; I walk in silence and gratitude, knowing that I have left a part of myself at the summit and that I will carry a part of it with me wherever I go.

5. *The return stage:* At the end of the day, I am usually quiet, almost pensive. I have taken my leave of the mountain and have turned my thoughts to other things; I am ready for home. Part of me, in fact, feels as though I am already there; something clicks inside of me and tells me that the journey is over, at least in spirit. As I get in my car and head back to the ordinary routine of daily life, a lulling peacefulness eventually comes over me. I find myself looking back at the day with a smile—and looking forward to a shave and a shower. Later, in the evening, I will eat a nice meal with family and friends, share my adventure with them (possibly the best part of the day), prepare for bed,

say my prayers, and fall asleep—ready to face whatever the new day might bring.

Preparation. Ascent. Rest. Descent. Return. Nothing is extraordinary in these actions. To my mind, however, they permeate every aspect of the human adventure. That is why mountains have such a strange, mysterious attraction. When we climb a mountain, our actions reflect back on us and help us see who we are, making the entire process a metaphor for the human journey. We prepare only to return; we ascend and eventually descend. We live the journey but often forget to rest along the way and look to where the sun touches the sky.

Mountains help us do this. They evoke in us the whole gamut of human emotions: from awe to dread, from a deep sense of wonder at the beauty and immensity of God's creation to a fear of being overwhelmed by nature's powerful, unwieldy forces. Mountains challenge us to raise our sights, yet make us tremble at the precarious movements of the winds that hound their towering summits. They call us to higher ground, yet bid us to watch our every move lest we stumble, fall, become disoriented, and lose our bearings.

The Spiritual Quest

What am I getting at? By now, I hope it should be obvious. Mountains inspire us to imagine the unimaginable, to rise to the heights or to fall to the lowest depths. They present us with a realm of possibility and challenge us—if we dare—to conquer their craggy rocks and cliffs simply because they lie in our path. From below, their lofty peaks summon us to reach for what lies beyond our grasp. From above, they remind us of how small we are in the vast, ever-unfolding scheme of the universe. Mountains humble us and exalt us. They cleanse us and sanctify us. They evoke from us all that is good as well as all that is horrifying.

Is it any wonder that saints and prophets journeyed to the tops of mountains to listen to God, to find God, to wrestle with God? It was in the rocky clefts of Mount Sinai, for example, that Moses received from Yahweh the tablets of the Law (see Exodus 19–20). It was high atop Mount Carmel that Elijah heard the voice of God not in the wind or the earthquake, but in a small whispering voice (see 1 Kings 19:9–17). It was on the lofty summit of Mount Tabor that Jesus, deep in the throes of prayer, revealed his majesty to his closest disciples (see Matthew 17:1–8). Where else but on the tops of mountains would such intimate yet awe-inspiring encounters of the human and the divine occur?

Mountains enkindle in us a sense of awe and wonder at the world and all its beauty. Without mountains, the human spirit would find it much more difficult to extend its arms and touch its deepest hopes; the world would be a much smaller place, and we would be very much the poorer. Mountains have a powerful sway over us. They speak to us on the deepest level of our experience. They represent all that is challenging, unconquerable, beyond our reach. They also represent the destructive power and cruelty of the elements.

Mountains touch our spiritual sensitivities and remind us of the fragility of life and the great unwieldy forces beyond our control. Whoever climbs a mountain cannot help but feel the deep upward movement of the human journey itself, an ascent often hindered by heartbreaking obstacles and shocking disappointments. Whoever espies the world from atop a lofty peak usually descends with a better sense of his or her place in that world. One does not return to the world below without marking the memory of this ascent somewhere deep within the heart. This memory nestles itself in the soul and provides one with strength and solace in whatever challenges may lie ahead.

Conclusion

Sometimes life passes by so quickly that it is difficult for us to remember the importance of making solid preparations for the future, of keeping our destination in view, of resting in the sheer joy of existence, of reflecting on what we have seen, and of sharing our experience with others. Whenever you find this is so, whenever you lose your bearings and life seems to have little sense or purpose, my advice to you would be simply this: "Go climb a mountain." I am sure you can locate one you would be able to handle, and you may well find the climb to be a rewarding experience, perhaps spiritually refreshing. Why? Because mountains keep alive our yearning for transcendence. Their simplicity, majesty, and beauty touch us deeply, remind us of what is best in the human heart, and inspire us to tap our deepest potential. We must have mountains in our lives, ones not so very far away, that we can manage. It is important that our mountains simply be there, even if we do nothing more than yearn for a view from their lofty peaks, climb them silently in our dreams, or contemplate them peacefully from a distance—and in the quiet of our hearts.

Reflection Questions

1. Do you ever take time to absorb the beauty of the world around you? Do you ever hike a trail, canoe down a river, climb a mountain? Would you have to travel far from home to enjoy such things? If so, would you consider taking a day or a weekend to enjoy the outdoors? If not, how often do you actually take advantage of such things? Are you refreshed by the outdoors? If so, in what ways?

2. Have you ever had an experience of awe? Where were you at that time? What brought it about? What other kinds of feelings did the experience spark in you? Did the experi-

ence last for a brief time? a long time? What kind of thoughts did it raise in you? Did the experience foster or diminish your faith? Did it make you feel ill at ease or did it fill you with gratitude?

3. Have you ever had a firsthand experience of the great destructive power of nature? If not, do you know anyone who has suffered deep personal loss as a result of a hurricane, flood, harsh winter storm, or the scorching summer heat? How do such tragedies affect people? Why are such tragedies permitted to happen? Does the power of nature frighten you? upset you? make you wary?

4. Where would you place yourself along your spiritual journey through life? in the preparation stage? the ascent stage? the resting stage? the descent stage? the return stage? Do you think any particular stage is more demanding than the others? If so, which one? Why?

5. Can you think of any other images or metaphors that describe the nature of your spiritual journey? Do these images come from nature? from your relationships? from your dreams? What are the strengths and weaknesses of the various images you have found? Does one stand out with particular clarity? Do the images complement one another? If so, how?

EXERCISE

Take a hike to the highest accessible point in your immediate vicinity: a mountain, a hill, the tower of a building. Even a small elevation will do. When you reach the top, look out in every direction: north, south, east, and west. Take note of what you see. Note the difference in perspective that allows you to see so much farther than you can see from the ground. Now close your eyes, look inside yourself, and imagine you are climbing the mountain of your soul. What kind of elevation is it? very high? intermediate? fairly low? Note the various stages of the journey as you ascend and descend the mountain of your soul: the preparation, the ascent, the time for rest, the descent, the return. Does anything in particular strike you? Try to describe it. When you finish, open your eyes and descend from the high point you were standing on. Return home, get out your Bible, and read the story of Jesus' Transfiguration (see Luke 9:29–36).

Book Ten
Spiritual Rhythms

Thou mastering me God!
giver of breath and bread;
World's strand, sway of the sea;
Lord of living and dead;
Thou hast bound bones and veins in me,
fastened me flesh,
And after it almost unmade,
what with dread,
Thy doing: and dost thou touch me afresh?
Over again I feel thy finger and find thee.

Gerard Manley Hopkins,
"The Wreck of the Deutschland"[20]

If you have ever attended the performance of a symphony orchestra and listened to the music elicited by a single maestro from so many different instruments, you have a good idea of what the action of prayer is like. We sustain our relationship with God through prayer. This activity begins and ends in God and involves the vast variety of instruments that makes us what we are: the physical, the emotional, the intellectual, the social, and the spiritual. Our unique relationship with God is nurtured through a rhythm of prayer that incorporates each of these important dimensions. That rhythm, however, must be genuine, one that fits our own unique personalities and allows us to be ourselves before God and neighbor.

The Physical

Our body is not a garment we wear or a mask we can simply put on and take off. Rather than conceal who we are, our body *reveals* who we are: to God, to others, and to the world around us. Our body forms an integral part of our human nature. It places us within the boundaries of space and time; sets the limits through which we live out our earthly lives; confronts us with the inevitability of death; and forces us to ponder the meaning of human mortality.

Our body can be oriented toward God and should play an important role in our life of prayer. It is important that, from time to time, we reflect on how we use our body to give praise and glory to God. What does this mean in the concrete world? For one thing, it means caring for our body, that is, making sure that we do not overwork it, that we give it enough rest and exercise, that we free it of any harmful or destructive habits. It also means listening to our body, that is, providing it with adequate nourishment to ward off hunger and thirst, giving it adequate medical treatment when illness renders it weak or incapacitated. Care of the body is intimately connected to care of the soul; the two should not be separated. A healthy relationship with God avoids anything that uplifts one at the expense of the other. Such an unhealthy dualism ultimately fragments our relationship to God by failing to allow us to bring all of who we are into our life of prayer.

We must bring our body with us when we pray. That is, we must allow our prayer to find some manner of concrete, physical expression. We can do this in any number of ways: through gestures and song, through vocal prayers, through movement and dance. We can also orient our body to God by denying it moderate amounts of the natural goods that sustain it (for example, food, drink, and sleep). Fast and abstinence, holy hours, and night vigils are ways in which Christians have traditionally offered praise and honor to God through their bodies. Through such sacrifices, we orient the physical side of our nature to God and thus render our act of worship more complete.

THE EMOTIONAL

We are more than just our body; our feelings are another important aspect of who we are. These, too, should be oriented toward God when we pray. To do this it is important for us to be in touch with them, to name them, to understand them, and to express them. Many of us were taught from an early age to mistrust our feelings, that they should not be openly expressed. Feelings, we were told, concern no one but ourselves; they are not to be hung out for public display and have little if anything to do with the way we pray. Such attitudes, wherever they came from—our parents, our teachers, our peer group, our culture—are misleading and, when left unchecked, can do great damage to our relationship with God.

Feelings represent one of the most private areas of our lives. When we reveal them to others, we make ourselves vulnerable and risk letting others see us as we really are. By expressing our feelings to God, we are not telling him anything new, of course; he already knows everything about us. Rather, we are expressing our own trust in his love for us. By getting in touch with our emotions—by naming our anger, sadness, fears, shame, hurts, and doubts, as well as our joys, desires, deepest hungers, and yearnings—and then sharing them with God, we invite him to be actively involved in the intimate details of our lives. Not to do so would be a sign that we do not entirely trust God. In effect, it would be like telling God that he can enter our world only to a certain point, beyond which we do not trust him—that there is a part of our lives that we wish to control and want no one else to see.

If we are afraid to look at our emotions and are not quite sure what to do with them, we most likely find it difficult to share our feelings with God. Bringing our feelings to prayer demands a great deal of honesty. It means taking the time to look at ourselves and allowing uncomfortable and sometimes threatening emotions to rise to the surface. By putting our feelings before God, we open the vulnerable side of our lives and allow him to help us sift through our emotions and integrate them with the rest of our lives.

The Intellectual

We are more than just the sum total of our biological processes and emotions. Reason and will also come into play—that side of us that enables us to think and understand, to imagine and remember, to choose and command. Most of us have little difficulty with the idea of turning our minds to God in prayer. We are comfortable on this level of who we are and recognize the importance of turning over to God this noble part of our human nature. Traditional forms of prayer such as meditation, *lectio divina,* and active contemplation are typically associated with this dimension of our anthropological makeup. Somehow we instinctively know that prayer must involve a turning of all of our mental powers to God and that, not to do so, closes off from God an important element of our human experience.

Turning our minds to God implies a willingness to share our innermost thoughts and deepest intentions. It means taking the time to exercise our minds with spiritual reading; to reflect on the events of the day in order to discern God's presence in our lives; to meditate upon the mysteries of Christ's Passion, death, and Resurrection; and to study the teachings of the Church so that they might become heartfelt convictions that guide us through life. It also means using our minds creatively to penetrate what the Church teaches about the mystery of God and to come up with new formulations that express the meaning of divine Revelation more clearly. Any use of the mind—be it reason, imagination, memory, or the will—that opens us up to the basic questions of existence and helps us enter into an ongoing conversation with the living God falls under this important dimension of prayer.

Care must be taken, of course, to not identify prayer exclusively with a movement of the intellect toward God. To do so would greatly downplay, perhaps entirely overlook, some of the other, equally important dimensions of prayer.

THE SOCIAL

In the past, we, too, often have thought of prayer as a private affair, as something individuals did on their own without any recourse to or input from other people. Prayer was something we did privately in our rooms, on our own time, when no one was watching. We even used Scripture to back up our assertions: "Whenever you pray, go to your room, close your door, and pray to your Father in private" (Matthew 6:6).

This attitude toward prayer, however, overlooks the fact that much of who we are is shaped by the people around us and the culture we live in. We are social by nature and cannot simply dismiss our capacity to enter into relationship with others. Our ability to forge bonds with others touches the very core of who we are; take that away and a huge, gaping hole opens up in the center of our being.

What can we do to help fill that hole? At appropriate times, we must turn to God in prayer not as individuals, but as a community of believers. So important is this communal dimension of our lives that some have gone so far as to say that God relates to us first as a people, and only secondarily as individuals. Group prayer, especially of the liturgical kind, is not something that can simply be discarded or thought of as unnecessary for a strong, healthy relationship with God. On the contrary, our relationship with God is engendered, nourished, and brought to its fullness within the life of the believing community. Eucharistic celebrations, prayer meetings, processions, common retreats, are all ways for us to give expression to this important corporate dimension of our lives.

The Spiritual

Finally, there is the spiritual dimension of our human makeup, the deepest side of who we are, the part that yearns to commune with God's Spirit, the part that groans with all creation as it awaits the fulfillment of God's promises. This side of us is most at home in silence. It likes to rest in quiet and listen to the faint whispers of the divine voice within us. There, our spirit communes with God; it rests in the gentle breeze of the Spirit and drinks from the refreshing waters it finds in the deepest recesses of the soul.

In holy silence, we rest with God in quiet contemplation. We open ourselves to the movement of the Spirit in our lives while we rest in the peaceful knowledge of its sanctifying and healing action. This gentle awareness of the divine deep within our heart gives us the assurance of God's ongoing presence in our life. Such an assurance comes not through the limitations of language, ideas, or formulations, but through direct contact with the power of God's Spirit who, in touching our own, reminds us of the destiny we are bound for and hope one day to reach.

The spiritual dimension of human existence reminds us to be quiet, to rest from our labors, and to allow God's Spirit to work within us in the still, deep-running waters of our soul. The spiritual dimension of our human makeup flows through and touches every other dimension of our existence. When we fail to orient our spirits toward God, all else within us—our physical labors, our emotional peace, our intellectual accomplishments, our social relationships—can easily come unraveled. Becoming a spiritual person thus means allowing God to help us find a moment of stillness in everything we do, regardless of the time, place, or circumstances. It means seeking God in all things and living in ways that allow the divine presence to move more and more to the forefront of our life.

A SUITABLE RHYTHM

Each of us must strive to find that particular rhythm of prayer that incorporates these five dimensions of human existence, although they may not always be present to the same degree. We are all unique individuals; there never was and never will be anyone else quite like each of us. Our relationship with God is also unique, containing a matchless quality that comes through most clearly in the particular blend of the physical, emotional, intellectual, social, and spiritual dimensions of our prayer. Each person's prayer contains a slightly different mixture of these five dimensions. One person will tend more toward the physical, another toward feeling, another toward the intellectual, the social, or the spiritual. One person may neglect one or more of these dimensions; another may incorporate all of them but to different degrees and with different shades of emphasis.

When at prayer, most of us turn more readily toward our strengths, those elements of our personal makeup that we feel most comfortable with. Outdoor types will find it much easier to give praise and glory to God through external, physical expressions (for example, plowing a field or chopping wood). Sensitive persons will feel more comfortable sharing their feelings with God. Intellectuals will find it much easier to pray by meditating or doing a *lectio divina*. Extroverts will feel most comfortable in a social gathering of prayer. Spiritual persons will want to gaze into an icon or simply rest in a chapel before the Blessed Sacrament.

Regardless of our individual preferences or natural leanings, each of these dimensions of human existence—the physical, emotional, intellectual, social, and spiritual—has a place in our relationship with God and should be taken into account. For this very reason, it is important for us to examine our life of prayer to see which dimensions we may be unwittingly—or perhaps consciously—omitting. The challenge is for each of us to look not so much to our strengths, but to our weaknesses as the place where we need to grow in our life of prayer. *Have I found a rhythm of prayer in my life that includes all five dimensions? Which of them, if any, am I failing to open up to God? What can I do to change the situation?* If we are genuinely interested in deepening our relationship with God, these are the kinds of questions we pose to ourselves. Not to do so could mean that we are holding something back from God.

The Rhythm of the Liturgy

These observations help us to see the Church's celebration of the liturgy (Eucharist, the sacraments, the Divine Office) in a different light. When at prayer, the Church provides time and space for each of these human dimensions to rise to the surface. Physical gestures, such as bowing and genuflecting, standing and sitting, raising arms to God and blessing ourselves and one another with the sign of the cross, demonstrate a concern for the physical. Sacred music inspires us with feelings of deep affection and devotion. Readings from Holy Writ and homilies that break them open for us nourish our minds and incite us to unite our hearts to Christ's. The communal gathering of believers as one Body in Christ manifests the social aspect of human existence. Appropriate moments of silence allow our spirits' Spirit to yearn within us and to be overshadowed by the divine.

When the Body of Christ gathers in prayer, each of these five dimensions should be present and acknowledged in a rhythm that manifests itself in not one but all the seasons of the liturgical year. Otherwise, something is lacking that prevents the Church from being *fully* at prayer; what is writ large in the official prayer of the Church will never fully incarnate itself in our daily lives.

CONCLUSION

It makes little sense to argue about which particular prayer form is superior or most appropriate to this or that stage of our spiritual journey. When discussing the role of prayer in our lives, we need to look at how we maintain a proper rhythm among the physical, emotional, intellectual, social, and spiritual dimensions of our human makeup—with a specific concentration on the dimensions we may be neglecting. The liturgy stands out as that prayer par excellence in which each of these important dimensions can and should be continually fostered. When examined in terms of the rhythm it engenders, its central role in our daily lives stands out for all to behold in a refreshing and innovative way.

REFLECTION QUESTIONS

1. Which dimension of who you are as a human being do you feel most comfortable with when you pray? the physical, emotional, intellectual, social, or spiritual? Might that particular dimension of human existence be your strong point? If so, in what other ways can you orient this particular strength toward God?

2. When it comes to prayer, which dimension would you consider your weak points? Why? Can you think of any ways you could develop this weakness so that it can become more integrated in your prayer life? Would you be willing to try them for a while? If not, why not?

3. Do you have a rhythm of prayer? How would you describe it? Does your particular rhythm of prayer come full circle in a single day? in the space of a couple of days? in a week? What could you do to strengthen the rhythm of prayer in your life so that it might become more and more deeply ingrained?

4. Do you experience a rhythm in the Church's liturgical celebrations? Do you find, for example, that each of the dimensions of human existence—the physical, emotional, intellectual, social, and spiritual—is nurtured when you gather for worship with other members of the believing community? How would you describe that rhythm? Does it in any way parallel your own rhythm of personal prayer? How could these two rhythms be brought more in sync with each other?

5. How would you describe your relationship with God? Does it involve all of the dimensions of human existence? Can you think of any other dimensions of human existence that could be included (for example, dreams, the unconscious)? Since there is an infinite number of dimensions in God, would you accept the possibility that the divine could manifest itself in our lives in ways we still are not able to fully comprehend? If not, why not?

EXERCISE

Listen to classical music, perhaps Mozart's *Symphony in D* or Bach's *Violin Concerto No. 1;* simply choose something you like. If you are not familiar with classical music, tune in a classical music station on your radio. Close your eyes and listen to the music. After a few minutes, try to determine how many different musical instruments are involved in the production. Can you name them? As the music continues, close your eyes and imagine that you are singing to God with every level of your being: physical, emotional, intellectual, social, and spiritual. Pretend you are the maestro of a great symphony that extends out from deep within your being, giving praise and glory to God. Can you sense the harmony and rhythm of the various dimensions of your being? What does your symphony sound like? How would you describe it? joyful? contemplative? angry? sad? Try to hum its various movements out loud. When you open your eyes, try to carry the various movements with you throughout the day.

Book Eleven

A Sign of Hope

i am a little church (no great cathedral)
far from the splendor and squalor of hurrying cities
—i do not worry if briefer days grow briefest,
i am not sorry when sun and rain make April.

E. E. CUMMINGS, 77[21]

Not long ago I made my way through the rolling hills and ripened vineyards of southern Burgundy in eastern France to a place recognized both far and wide as one of the world's great spiritual centers: the monastic community of Taizé. Founded in 1940 by a young Swiss theologian named Roger Schultz, the monastery began as a valiant attempt to restore monastic practice to the Protestant faith. It soon blossomed into a truly ecumenical venture that has since attracted members from Catholic and Protestant backgrounds alike from over twenty countries.

Located atop a small hill in the vicinity of Sâone-et-Loire, not far from the ramshackle ruins of Cluny, that great center of Benedictine monasticism that helped carve so much of the spiritual and temporal landscape of medieval Europe, Taizé represents a vital resurgence of the monastic spirit, the likes of which have not been seen in Western society for many, many years. Known for its simplicity of life, its calming musical rounds, and its warm hospitality to strangers (especially the young), the community of Taizé has succeeded in blending old and new, the concerns of past and present, in a way that has awakened the deep spiritual sensibilities of our anxiety-ridden world. No wonder it has become a veritable Mecca for many of those who wish to satisfy the latent pains of humanity's deep spiritual hungers.

HUNGER AND DUST

Taizé's rustic environment does not encourage visits from the weak and feeble of heart. Those who enter its grounds must be prepared to forego many of the comforts of home they normally take for granted. The basic necessities are provided—to be sure—but not much more. The wooden barracks, the earthen trails, the open-air refectory, and the simple fare of lentils, bread, juice, and fruit remind weary travelers that they come to this holy place for one purpose and one purpose only—to search for God.

The young, in particular, are attracted by Taizé's austere regimen of life. Since 1957 they have flocked there by the thousands to feed their souls on its simple fare and sound spiritual sustenance. They come, in part, to escape the materialism and confusion of a tension-filled world; in part, to understand the meaning of their difficult (and often bewildering) journey through life; in part, to fathom the uncharted depths of their inner yearning for God and, more importantly, of God's intense and deeply compassionate longing for them.

Two things in particular struck me when I arrived there tired and hungry on a sun-dried autumn day: (1) the dust from the trails that, during the course of the day, had been kicked up by thousands of visitors (it apparently had not rained for quite some time), and (2) the long lines at mealtime (even simple fare needs time to be distributed to such a large crowd). These two details have come to dominate my impression of Taizé. Together, they tell of the great success of this extraordinary experiment in monastic living and show how it now stands at the crossroads of Europe's long and rather circuitous spiritual journey. Hungry pilgrims, covered with dust, waiting to be fed lentils and bread. Hungry, but happy—and more than willing to wait their turn.

Given its Spartan fare, its cramped quarters, its vulnerability to the elements, and its many other physical restrictions, Taizé seems a long way from the primeval garden of our dreams; an earthly paradise it obviously is not! Nor does it purport to be. To the naked eye, Taizé seems very much like a plain, ordinary, even uninviting *place*. So why, we might ask, does anyone go there? Certainly not for the food or the primitive shelter it offers. Certainly not to walk the heavily rutted trails or to inhale the dusty air that envelops them and sticks to their clothes. Something else has surely drawn them.

In Praise of God

That something else can be found in the Church of the Reconciliation, the spiritual center of the Taizé community, where day after day pilgrims join the small gathering of white-robed monks in raising their hearts and voices to God. The Taizé office combines different styles of liturgical music into a simple but eloquent offering of praise. Great care is taken not only to train visitors in the various rounds and harmonies that form the backbone of the liturgy but also to utilize the talents (musical or otherwise) of everyone present. The results impress even the most detached observer—and with good reason.

A typical celebration will find a thousand or so silent pilgrims sitting quietly in prayerful expectation for the monks to process in silent devotion and take their positions at the prayer stools that line the choir space down the center of the church. At the end of the procession, Brother Roger takes his place at the head of the community and gathers around him his special guests, any children who have come there for the service: "Let the children come to me.... The kingdom of God belongs to such as these" (Matthew 19:14). The pregnant silence then gives way to antiphonal praise, usually in the form of a simple round that has been carefully rehearsed the day before: "*Ubi caritas et amor....*" The harmony of voices fills the church and transforms its simple and functional surroundings into vibrating and living movement of the Spirit. Suddenly the music ends and silence once more reverberates throughout the interior spaces of the soul. All eyes are focused on the large flowing banners of red and orange colors in the front of the sanctuary that present the participants with simple yet powerful symbols of the spiritual Pentecost they have all come to receive.

The small voice of a child then calls out in the wilderness of the heart. "Prepare the way of the Lord" (John 1:23). A lesson from Scripture follows as the moments continue to brush with eternity and the community of believers experiences its oneness in Christ on a level never known before. There is then another round of chant, more silence, and another lesson from Scripture. One's consciousness of time quietly recedes.

Before you know it, it is time to conclude, and the passage from the Life of the Liturgy to the Liturgy of Life takes place with joyous expectation. A strong sense pervades the congregation that something good has been done for God and for the health of the soul. Its collective inner longings now seem focused anew, even strangely transformed, and people leave the Church of the Reconciliation somehow more in touch with their own inner brokenness, with the brokenness of the Church, with the brokenness of the world. Yet, they carry with them a strong confidence in a God who is with them as they journey beyond the bounds of Taizé, trusting that he will not only help them but also bind them up and heal their wounds.

An Ecumenical Vision

The beauty of Taizé lies in its hearty and welcoming embrace of all who seek to follow the narrow and winding way of the Lord Jesus. This simple hand of friendship extended to every Christian, regardless of his or her confessional background or religious affiliation, has enabled the community to play an important role in the ecumenical movement on both theological and popular levels. In return for its offer of hospitality, the community of Taizé, which does not accept gifts or donations of any kind, asks only that believers focus on what unites them, not on what separates them. In doing so, it hopes to overcome centuries of doctrinal misunderstanding, bitter (often brutal) polemics, and deep mutual suspicion.

According to the Taizé philosophy, only an atmosphere of trust and free, open dialogue will help Christian churches overcome their longstanding divisions of faith. The community of monks, itself comprised of ordained and nonordained members of various Catholic and Protestant backgrounds, eagerly looks forward to the day when Christians everywhere will be able to partake freely in the eucharistic banquet and rejoice in the presence of Jesus in their midst. It recognizes that the road to unity is long and difficult but it is confident, nonetheless, that Jesus is with them at every turn and that his will for them is to walk the path to unity in open and humble respect for the truth. As it does so, it continues its quiet sojourn through time by singing the praises of the Lord and responding dutifully to the presence of the Spirit in its midst.

Such a response has led the community to send some of its members to the poverty-stricken areas of Asia, Africa, Eastern Europe, and the Americas, to bring the spirit and message of Taizé to those who are too poor to journey to its monastery door. The result has been a great proliferation of its spirit throughout the world, a great spiritual work that is also nurtured through its widespread distribution of books, tapes, religious artifacts, and other expressions of the Taizé way of life.

CONCLUSION

The monks of Taizé offer the Church an alternative vision of monastic life, one that looks beyond the divisions that presently separate Christians to the day when the Lord's quiet rule of peace will take hold of their mutual relations. Their life together points to the day when their hope will become reality. Bound by the vows of celibacy, community of goods, and submission to the authority of the prior, the monks offer the Church a living testimony of the transforming power of hope, a power, they believe, will one day convert the scandal of division into an outpouring of the Spirit in the form of a Second Pentecost. As the world steps into a new millennium, the monks of Taizé remind the Church of the urgent missionary import of Jesus' impassioned prayer for unity: "I pray that they may be one in us, that the world may believe that you sent me" (John 17:21). Unity of mind and heart among Christians will do much to convince the world of the authenticity of Jesus' claims—for only Jesus and the power of his Spirit can effect such a radical transformation in the life of the believing community.

My visit to Taizé strengthened my own desire to walk further down the road toward Christian unity and to explore its practical options in the concrete circumstances of my religious convictions. It also enkindled in me a deeper awareness of the Spirit's unique role as an instrument of that fragile peace that the world cannot impart. At the end of my time there, I felt that I had witnessed a movement of the Spirit that extended far beyond the boundaries of that small hilltop in eastern France.

Taizé, and what it stands for, captured my imagination as it had already penetrated the minds and hearts of countless others before me. This small community of prayerful, dedicated monks has had a great impact on a divided Church and the world it so desperately yet, for some strange reason, so hesitantly wishes to serve. "O God, you are my God, for you I long" (Psalm 63:2). The cry of the psalmist resounds not only in the life of this humble gathering of monks, but in the hearts of all who have spent time with them, worshiped with them, and listened to their heartfelt and deeply spiritual message of hope.

Reflection Questions

1. Have you ever gone on a pilgrimage? Where did you go? Was it a rewarding experience? Did it help you spiritually in any way? What do you think attracts people to leave their homes and familiar surroundings to travel, sometimes long distances, to a site such as Taizé?

2. Why are the young so attracted to Taizé? Is it the monastery's rugged simplicity? its simple fare? its welcoming atmosphere? its good singing? its sense of celebration? its ecumenical dimension? Are you attracted to it in any way? Do you think you could benefit from such a journey? Why?

3. Have you ever attended an ecumenical worship service? Did you benefit from it? Did it change your outlook toward other Christian faiths? If so, in what ways? Did it change your outlook toward the members of other faiths? If so, in what ways? What new insights does a community like Taizé bring to the ecumenical discussion? Does it present any dangers?

4. How would you describe Taizé spirituality? Why have its music and worship services become so popular? Is it because of the community's simplicity? its contemplative at-

titude toward life? the way it makes the monastic tradition of the Christian religion available to the people at large? Would you ever be interested in attending such a service in a local church or prayer group?

5. In what ways is Taizé a sign of hope for Christians of the new millennium? What values does it seek to convey? Do you share in those values? Do you see the Taizé community as a sign of hope? What is the community pointing toward? What is it trying to bring about at this important juncture in history? Can you think of any concrete ways in which you could participate in this vision?

EXERCISE

Sing one of the Taizé chants like "*Ubi caritas.*" If you don't know it, try to get a tape of it or have someone teach you one of the chants. They are well known and easy to learn. Begin by singing the chant in a low voice for about five to ten minutes. When you reach the end of the chant, go back and start again. When five or ten minutes are up, remain sitting in silence, and try not to think of anything but the words and the music of the chant. Breathe in, breathe out, and let the chant fill your soul and penetrate your mind and spirit. After another five minutes, start chanting again, this time with a louder voice. Sing the chant with all your heart, mind, soul, and strength. Then thank the Lord for Taizé and all it stands for.

Book Twelve

PRAYING THE PSALMS

Bless the Lord, O my soul;
and all my being, bless his holy name.
Bless the Lord, O my soul,
and forget not all his benefits;
He pardons all your iniquities,
he heals all your ills.
He redeems your life from destruction,
he crowns you with kindness and compassion.
He fills your lifetime with good;
your youth is renewed like the eagle's.

PSALM 103:1–5[22]

A young woman, rising half an hour earlier than she really needs to, opens the window to let in the fresh morning air and then sits in a chair next to her bed. She turns on the lamp on her night table, takes out a small prayer book, opens it to the place she had marked the night before, and begins her morning prayer: "Lord, open my lips, and my mouth will proclaim your praise." Quietly and meditatively, the young woman reads the three psalms of lauds, followed by a brief reading, a gospel canticle, some closing intercessions, the Lord's Prayer, and a concluding prayer; it takes about fifteen minutes. When she is finished, she closes her eyes and rests in quiet for a few minutes, allowing the words of Scripture to sink deeply into her heart. When she opens her eyes, she is ready to get on with her day. She does so not alone, but as a member of Christ's Body, the Church.

PRAYER OF THE CHURCH

The Psalms are an integral part of the Church's Liturgy of the Hours. When we recite or sing them, or meditate upon them alone or in common, we do so not as individuals, but as members of Christ's Body. As Christians, we pray the Psalms with the understanding that Christ is the fullness of God's revelation to us and that his coming was mysteriously foreshadowed in the insights and inspirations of the psalmist. For this reason, the words of the Psalms have special significance for us. In them, we find a reflection of our relationship to Jesus and of Jesus' relationship to the Father. When we pray the Psalms, we do so through, with, and in Christ, who is Emmanuel—"God with us"—and we discover that Christ is, in fact, "with us" in a variety of ways.

1. *In the day:* The Psalms form the major part of the seven "hours" of the Divine Office and are an important way for us to offer the day to God and make it holy. This tradition is deeply rooted in our Catholic tradition, dating back to *The Rule of Saint Benedict* and its attempt to help small communities of monks sanctify their day through work, prayer, and spiritual reading. Although we live in a very different age and cultural milieu, our present use of the Psalms is not all that different. By taking time to pray the Psalter each day, we orient to God all that comes both before and after our time of prayer. In doing so, we recognize that Christ is with us not only as we pray but also as we carry out the rest of our daily activities. In this way, the Psalms gather our innermost desires to offer everything in our lives to God.

2. *In the body:* The Psalms were meant to be sung and, at times, danced. They call for physical expression, even if we simply recited them out loud, or sit or kneel in meditative fashion when we pray them. By exercising our bodies in this way, we underscore the fundamental goodness of the material world and God's promise through Christ of the ongoing sanctification of our bodies. Christ is with us in our bodily existence as we worship God with singing voices and uplifted arms. Our praises blend with his as we give honor and glory to God. Our bodily acts of worship concretize our belief that God has come to redeem *all* of who we are. Without these concrete, physical gestures, something would be missing from the homage we pay to God, as if to say that some part of our existence is excluded from Christ's redemptive action or, worse yet, beyond the pale of God's compassionate love.

3. *In the emotions:* The Psalms cover a wide range of emotions: fear, hope, joy, sadness, anger, depression, trust, betrayal, thanksgiving, praise—to name but a few. When we pray the Psalms, we get in touch with our own feelings and turn them over to Christ. Like us in every way (Hebrews 2:17), Christ plumbs the depths of human experience and understands our emotions from the inside looking out. Not only does he understand them, he experiences them himself and elevates them to another plane by purifying them and sanctifying them in his prayer to the Father. In this way, he unites our prayer to his and brings us further along the slow, gradual process of divinization.

4. *In the mind:* The precise meaning of the Psalms is not always clear to us. Written so long ago and in a historical and cultural setting so very different from our own, the Psalms need to be pondered and meditated upon if we are to discover their relevance for our lives. The Psalms chal-

lenge our minds first to penetrate their external shell and then to chew upon and digest their latent spiritual meanings. Christ is with us as we explore the depths of these ancient hymns and discover their hidden treasures. He accompanies us on our journey beneath their literal sense to the significance they hold for us in our daily walk through life. Our minds are both strengthened and sensitized in the process; they become prone to delving beneath the surface of things to find rest and solace in the quiet matters the heart.

5. *In community:* Because of their extensive use in the Liturgy, the Psalms are often referred to as the "prayer book of the Church." Because we are social beings by nature; because Christ promises to be present wherever two or three of us are gathered in his name (see Matthew 18:20); because we are members of Christ's Body, the Church; because the Psalms form a part of the Church's official prayer, that is, the Liturgy of the Hours: For these reasons, Christ is present with us when we gather in his name and pray, and the Psalms are an important means through which the Church gathers to celebrate the gift of community. The Psalms provide a focal point in and through which we are able to celebrate Christ's ongoing presence in our midst. Whenever we pray the Psalms, we do so united with all of the members of Christ's Body throughout the world.

6. *In the Spirit:* Last but certainly not least, the Psalms provide us with a means of contemplation. When we pray the Psalms, we enter the depths of our being, where our spirits are able to turn their gaze upward and commune with the Spirit of God. On this level, we pray the Psalms not merely with our lips or with mental images and concepts, but with our hearts. Here we encounter Christ in the depths of our soul and appreciate all the more the backdrop of silence that makes the

recitation of the Psalms possible. The pregnant pauses between the various antiphons and stanzas enable us to rest in the presence of the Spirit deep within our hearts, where we can hear the still small voice of God beckon us to partake in the mystery of divine love.

Conclusion

The Psalms touch us on every level of our existence. Whenever we pray the Psalms, we affirm our belief in the power of Christ to meet us where we are and to be with us in our continuing journey through life. The Psalms remind us that prayer must encompass every aspect of who we are and that all of us are called to love God with all our heart, mind, soul, and strength (see Luke 10:27). When we pray the Psalms, Christ prays with us to the Father in the Spirit. His prayer embraces our own and confirms us as members of his Body, the Church. The Psalms make explicit the deepest yearnings of our hearts and help us render to God the glory and praise he deserves. They bind us together more firmly in the peace of Christ's Spirit and enable us to participate more deeply in the mystery of his redeeming love.

Reflection Questions

1. Do you pray the Psalms regularly? hardly at all? once in a while? Do you pray them alone? with others? Do you think of the Psalms as the prayer of the Church universal? Do the Psalms have an important place in your spiritual life? Could you nurture your relationship with the Lord just as easily without the Psalms?

2. Do you find some of the Psalms more meaningful than others? Which ones are most meaningful to you? Why do you feel more drawn to some Psalms than to others? Do

the Psalms you favor tell you something about yourself? about others? about your image of God?

3. How do you pray the Psalms? Do you do so on every level of your being? Do you find that some Psalms address one dimension of human existence more than the others? Do you find that you tend to neglect some of the Psalms precisely for that reason?

4. Do you see any value in the use of a breviary format that ensures that all 150 Psalms are covered in a given amount of time? Do you consider the Psalms a valid way to offer continual praise to God? Can you think of any other ways in which such praise can be offered?

5. Can you think of a practical way of integrating the Psalms into your life of prayer? What would that entail? Would you be willing to implement these small steps into your daily rhythm of prayer? When would you be willing to start? Today?

EXERCISE

Open the Scriptures to the Book of Psalms. Pick one, not necessarily your favorite but one with which you are familiar. Read the psalm slowly and thoughtfully, and then read it again with careful attention to the various thoughts and emotions that the psalmist is trying to convey. Make a list of those thoughts and emotions (there is probably more than one), and then read the psalm again. When you finish, write your own prayer to God. Try to convey the thoughts and emotions that you presently experience, whatever they may be; be honest with yourself and with God. When you finish writing your prayer, read it out loud to God. If you can, think up a simple melody for your prayer and sing it aloud.

Book Thirteen

BLESSED INTERIORS

Who's at my window, who, who?
Go from my window, go, go!
Who calleth there so like a stranger?
Go from my window—go!
Lord, I am here, a wretched mortal
That for Thy mercy does cry and call—
Unto Thee, my Lord Celestial,
See who is at my window, who.

JOHN WEDDERBURN, "WHO'S AT MY WINDOW?"[23]

Not long ago I visited the cathedral of Notre Dame in Chartres. That was not, by any means, my main reason for being in France, nor was I particularly excited about the visit on that particular hot summer day in the middle of August. I was simply following the advice of friends who had been there themselves and who encouraged me to go if I ever had the opportunity. Having heard of the cathedral's famed stained glass and of its exquisite high Gothic architecture, I half expected my visit to resemble that of a visit to a museum: taking a tour of the grounds, noting the various stages of the cathedral's construction, going off on my own to examine some of the finer specimens of artwork and statuary still preserved there, and then eventually returning to the group. I certainly did not expect to have a deep experience of faith, so what I discovered took me completely by surprise.

ON THE OUTSIDE

One hazy Saturday morning I made the forty-minute journey by train out of Paris' Gare du Nord. As I got closer to my destination, I was impressed by the way the cathedral towered over everything else in the town and surrounding countryside. Chartres was still a relatively small town and, even though it was so very close to Paris, it had managed to maintain a strong sense of its medieval heritage. Its cathedral stands proudly on the highest point of the town and can be seen for miles against the rolling cornfields of the Beauce and various branches of the Eure River. As the train approached the town, I imagined the deep impression the sight would have made on medieval pilgrims as they made their way by foot and could see it off in the distance silhouetted against the evening sky. It must have seemed like paradise to them, as though a part of the heavenly Jerusalem had reached down and dignified them with its presence. That, at least, is how I think I would have felt.

When I actually stood in front of the cathedral and walked around it for the first time, however, my estimation of it went down sharply. Buildings are sometimes much more impressive from a distance than up close; once you are standing next to one, your impression of it can suddenly change. What from a distance seemed towering or awe-inspiring loses its sense of mystery and seems much more dull and commonplace. You squint your eyes and try to pretend you still see it as it appeared from a distance, even though you are only a few yards away. This attempt to accommodate rarely works, however. You normally end up opening your eyes and finding that what you had imagined has existed only in your mind and perhaps in the minds of those who built it. Close up you see the structures imperfections, the wear and tear that the wind and rain have caused down through the years, the slight imbalances in the architectural plan that make you want to rethink your initial impression—and so you do.

That is not to say that the exterior of Chartres does not impress. If it did not, it never would have been used by many other medieval towns as a model for their own houses of worship. The master builder of this late-twelfth and early-thirteenth century cathedral certainly knew what he was doing and seems to have matured as he got older. To this day, the south tower is considered a masterful architectural achievement, with its strong vertical lines and the use of dormer windows to change its shape from square to octagonal and then to an inverted conical shape. Equally impressive are the way the flying buttresses are integrated in the overall plan of the cathedral, thus allowing for thinner walls and a more lavish use of stained glass. The statuary, moreover, remains among the best medieval Europe had yet produced. There was more than enough on the cathedral's exterior to keep my attention fixed, and my guidebook helped me to appreciate the finer details of the cathedral's design even more.

Despite all of these absorbing points of interest, however, my first impression remained considerably dwindled. Why? Because deep in my heart I could not help but sense that somewhere, somehow, I had seen all of this before. On that particular day, I simply was not in the mood for taking in yet another dusty monument from the past, regardless of how well preserved and renowned it was. Sensing a boring day ahead, I decided to step inside, walk down the nave, across the transcript, tarry there for a while, leave, find a good restaurant, and eventually head home. Chartres was not the first cathedral I had visited in Europe that summer, and I had the sense that the rest of my visit would not show me anything I had not already seen many times before.

ON THE INSIDE

As soon as I stepped inside, however, I knew I was wrong. As I walked through the center portal of the western facade, I was immediately enveloped by a outspread cloak of colored light. The sun shone through the stained glass, casting all shapes and sizes of glowing light across the nave. It took a few moments for my eyes to adapt to the cathedral's darkened interior, but once I could see clearly, I could do nothing but marvel at the lively display of color all around me. Never before had I been immersed in such a beautiful work of art. The immense walls of glass seemed like sparkling jewels placed there by God not simply for adornment, but to manifest something of his majesty and glory.

As I stood in awe of what I was experiencing, I realized how the stained glass was perfectly complemented by the architecture, and that the master builder of the cathedral was using all knowledge at his disposal to build a veritable cathedral of light. My thoughts went back to what I knew about the medieval scholastics and the important role "light" played in their metaphysics. I also thought of their love of order and harmony and realized that what I was seeing was the architectural equivalent to the great theological *summae* of the thirteenth century; I even wondered if Thomas Aquinas had ever visited this cathedral.

Having been erected over the span of twenty-six years (1194–1220), the structure would have been completed a few years before Thomas's birth. I wondered if he ever had the opportunity to journey there during his student days in Paris or perhaps later, during one of his regencies as a university professor. Maybe; maybe not. Whatever the case, I am sure he would have felt quite at home in this spectacular interior which was meant to convey a sense of mystery and awe, all permeated by translucent shapes of multicolored lights. He would have been attracted by the Dionysian themes chosen for many of the windows, as well as by the exquisite sense of harmony and order portrayed in the ribbed vaults of the central nave. I now understood what was meant when his greatest work, the *Summa theologiae*, was likened to the carefully planned thrusts and counter thrusts of a Gothic cathedral. Whenever I think of Aquinas's *capolavoro*, the cathedral of Chartres now always comes to mind. Both are masterpieces; both are fascinating syntheses of old and new; both give witness to the beauty and truth of the Christian faith.

I abandoned my original plan to do a quick tour, find a restaurant, and head home. Instead, I stayed inside the cathedral for hours, moving here and there, from one set of window panels to the next, sitting down when I got tired or wanted to reflect on the amazing array of stories that were being told through their colorful imagery. I was especially fortunate because a recently established fund had allowed for some of the windows to be cleaned. I was thus able to see the difference between those still covered with the smut of centuries and those that were freshly cleaned—and the difference was amazing.

The cathedral has some of the most beautiful stained glass windows ever made. The light flaxen blue colors contrast wonderfully with the brilliant reds and dazzling whites to make up scenes from the Bible, the historical purpose of which was to instruct the illiterate masses who had no other way of understanding or passing on their faith. It struck me that in these mysterious frames the Book of the Word and the Book of Creation had here somehow become inextricably intertwined. I imagined the common folk mesmerized before the scenes of Christ's life, death, and Resurrection found at the three lancets on the western front. I tried to imagine an old peasant bringing his family to these windows and pointing out the various details of the gospel story.

As I wandered around the interior of the cathedral, with the excitement of a child who had so many toys that she could not decide which one to play with, I eventually found myself sitting before the recently cleaned panels of Jesus' parable of the Prodigal Son. I simply sat there and meditated on the story from one scene to the next, feeling as though Jesus himself were narrating it. The plot was the same, but the imagery, the characters, the climax, the meaning of the story, came through with such force and clarity that I felt as though I were hearing it for the very first time. I sat there for what seemed like hours, watching the lighting change with the movement of the sun and the shadows slowly extending themselves across the aisles. My prodigal heart came out from under the shadows of cynicism and doubt, returned to its senses, and went home. When a tear ran down my cheek and touched the corner of my mouth, I wiped it away with my hand and smiled. I felt welcomed here in this quiet church. I wanted to stay forever.

I eventually got up and walked to the rose window over the northern entrance, then to the one over the southern entrance, and finally to the one over the western entrance. As I pondered the scenes of the Last Judgment and of the life of the Blessed Virgin and the prophets, it came to me that everything in the cathedral was artistically and aesthetically arranged to assist the believer in contemplating the truths of faith. Everywhere I went I felt as though God were speaking to me, and I listened with my heart. As I gazed upon these scenes, I wondered what God might be trying to say to me, there, in that moment. When closing time came and I stepped out into the cool evening air to make my way back to the train station, I had a sense of what it might be.

UNDERSTANDING THE FAITH

The Christian faith is not all that different from a cathedral like Chartres. From a distance it looks impressive to the beholder and stirs the imagination. As we approach it and get up close, however, we begin to see its humanness, its imperfections, its frailties, its weaknesses. Seeing the exterior blemishes, we are disappointed and refuse to go inside to explore the inner sanctums of the faith.

Imperfections can be analyzed thoroughly from without, and we may even have an excellent idea about the concepts that support the faith. We will never appreciate the beauty of the faith and understand the truth it is trying to express, however, unless we step inside and see for ourselves. Once there, the faith takes on entirely different dimensions. Its height and depth, its texture, shape, and color: All come alive and dazzle us with a deep sense of God's presence in the mystery that surrounds us. We come to realize that the external structures of the faith are necessary, but exist only to the extent that they allow us to enter and experience the faith from within. We understand, moreover, that faith is more than an aesthetic experience, that all the time and craftsmanship that go into making such beautifully colored windows are nothing more than God's way of bringing out the deepest potential of creation itself.

Finally, we appreciate God's direct role in the experience of faith. That is to say that what we construct with our minds or with our hands will not attain its purpose unless the golden rays of the sun are permitted to shine through them and thus reveal to us the power and glory of the divine. "All else is as straw," as Aquinas put it.

Notre Dame of Chartres bids us to enter its walls and perceive the faith from within. It tells us to rejoice in what we are able to do for the greater glory of God, but it cautions us never to confuse that with the brilliance of the sun itself, whose golden rays alone allow the colors of its windows to sing, to dance, to make music, to rejoice, and to play in the deepest chambers of the human heart.

CONCLUSION

Sometimes our experience of something far exceeds our expectations. Such was the case with my trip to the cathedral of Notre Dame of Chartres. Such, I believe, can be the case with the experience of the faith as well. We live in an age when faith is scrutinized from every conceivable angle and is often presented as a "non-choice" for those who really wish to take life seriously. Such a position, to my mind, could not be any further from the truth and even borders on the tragic.

To those who relish an intense rationalist criticism of the faith, my response is: Go spend some time on the interior. Try to imagine what it might be like to believe. Bathe in the vivid colors of the gospel stories. Watch people's lives change as they allow the Word of God to touch their souls and penetrate the deepest recesses of their hearts. Do not remain on the outside. Rather, dare to live life from the inside out. Experience the faith from within. Let it speak to your heart. Otherwise, you will never understand what it means to believe, and all of your arguments, however strong they may seem at the time, will ultimately fail to convince.

Why? Because the human heart understands what the mind cannot comprehend. The human heart makes room for mystery, is able to converse with mystery, can be touched by mystery, is open to being transformed by mystery. A whole generation of medieval townsfolk spent their lives building a cathedral in Chartres that is now a lasting legacy to the deepest longings of their hearts. What they have left behind can also help mediate in our lives today a similar experience of faith. It is there and will remain there, but for the asking.

Reflection Questions

1. Do your expectations of an upcoming event usually exceed the event itself? Has it ever been the other way around: with the event itself far exceeding your expectations? Have you ever visited a place, met a person, saw a movie, or read a book that far exceeded your wildest dreams of what it would be like? Has anything like that ever happened in your life of faith?

2. How do you deal with imperfection in yourself? in others? in the Church? in God? Have you often found it to be a matter of what you perceive these imperfections to be? Do you ever find that you have been mistaken? Are you patient with the imperfections you find both within and without the faith?

3. Does it make sense to you that the faith must be experienced from within rather than analyzed from without? What are the strengths of such a position? What are the weaknesses? Would it be possible to experience the faith from both within and without? How might you deal with any resulting conflicts?

4. Is the harmony of the faith as found in the architectural and artistic achievement of Chartres a mere relic of the past? Does it have any relevance for faith today? What might that be? What message does a place like Chartres hold out for today's believers? What can Christians experience in a place like Chartres that they would have a difficult time finding elsewhere?

5. How does one convey a sense of the faith "from the inside out"? How can a believer communicate a sense of what it means to believe to someone who does not believe? What

role does prayer play in such an activity? What role does God play? How do you know when to cease your efforts and to let the illuminating light of God take over?

EXERCISE

Make a visit to a nearby church, preferably one with stained-glass windows. Walk around the outside of the church first. Observe its architecture, the materials it is made of, whatever improvements need to be made, how the grounds are kept, and so forth. Before stepping inside, look up and see if the sky is sunny or overcast. Once inside, look at the interior as a whole, then look specifically at the sanctuary lamp and then at the stained-glass windows (if there are any). Sit down in one of the pews, close your eyes, and imagine that *you* are the church you have just examined. Imagine that God is looking at you very closely: first from without, then from within. Try to get in touch with your feelings as you sense God examining every nook and cranny of your soul, especially when he stops before the sanctuary lamp of your soul and the colored windows through which the divine light shines.

Book Fourteen

HUMBLE ASKING

Ask, and you will receive.
Seek, and you will find.
Knock, and it will be opened to you.
For the one who asks, receives.
The one who seeks, finds.
The one who knocks, enters.

MATTHEW 7:7–9[24]

An old man leaves a cold stormy night behind, enters a dark, empty church, crosses himself, and enters the last row of pews. He kneels and bows his head in silence, heavy of mind and heart, not knowing how to begin or what to say. Tears roll down his face as he tries to remember the last time he was in a church; he can't recall.

Life has brought the man to his knees, to this church, and to his God. He has so many things to say but is afraid to open his mouth. It has been so long since he prayed to God, he barely remembers how. He thinks of all the things that have gone wrong in his life, of all the people he has hurt, of all the hurts he has endured. He wants to lay bare his heart before God but does not know how. He wants to give God his bodily and spiritual needs but wonders if he will be heard. Minutes pass as he buries his face in his hands and wipes his tears.

Eventually, the man raises his head and looks out into the darkness, toward the sanctuary lamp near the front of the church. Seeing the red light flickering near the tabernacle, he is reminded that he is in the presence of the Holy. He takes a deep breath and, letting the tears flow freely, he asks God pardon for his sins. Gradually, a great panoply of others follow this single request as the man, his tongue now loosened, is able to bare his needs and speak to his God from his heart.

A CARING GOD

So much of Christian prayer has to do with asking. Jesus, in fact, encouraged his disciples to bring their every need to God, their "Abba, Father" (see Matthew 6:9). He insisted that God would not give a stone to someone asking for bread, or a serpent to someone asking for a fish (see Matthew 9–10). "Ask, and you will receive. Seek, and you will find" (Matthew 7:7). The Gospels are full of examples of people asking Jesus for help. In Mark's Gospel alone, for example, there is the leper who seeks a cure (see 1:40), the paralytic in need of wholeness (see 2:1–12), the man whose daughter is sick (see 5:21–24), the woman with the hemorrhage (see 5:25–34)—and many more. Even the Our Father, the Christian prayer par excellence, asks us to bring our basic daily needs to God. If all this is true, why, then, do so many of us have a difficult time asking God for help when we need it? What is it that holds us back from doing what we should? Why are we afraid of storming heaven with our deepest and most intensely personal requests?

For many of us, our hesitation has to do with some of the exaggerated (if not distorted) images of God we have rolling around in our heads. If, for example, we picture God as an exacting judge who looks for and punishes our every mistake, we are not about to share with him our deepest needs and desires. Rather, we would prefer to hide our needs lest he take them for weakness or, worse yet, some kind of moral failure. For such a God, the less he knows the better. Why express our innermost thoughts and desires if they could one day be used against us? Many of us act this way on a gut, emotional level, even though we understand full well that God already knows us through and through. Ironically, we try to hide from God what God already knows. Why? Because we are afraid of what he will ask of us or, worse yet, *do* to us if we own up to the truth about ourselves.

In the same way, few of us would bring our needs to God if we sincerely thought he was much too busy to be bothered. If God is indifferent to our needs, it makes no sense to trouble him with the nitty-gritty details of our lives. If we know ahead of time that someone is simply going to ignore us, why bother talking to that person in the first place? The same is true for the way we speak to God. If we believe he is indifferent toward us, we will tend to be indifferent toward him—and to those around us. The same holds if we think of God as a remote impersonal force that rules the universe but not our hearts. It would be futile to express our needs to such a God; an impersonal force will not listen to, let alone answer, our prayers. No, we need a personal, loving God for that—and one not of our own making.

A Relational God

"[B]y prayer of petition we express awareness of our relationship with God." This insight from *The Catechism of the Catholic Church* (no. 2629) highlights the relational character of Christian prayer, that is, the Christian's belief that God can be not only addressed but also listened to, heard, and responded to. Bringing God our needs—all of them, from the loftiest to the most mundane—implies that we are already aware of his personal presence in our lives. That presence may seem distant, very close, or somewhere in between. However it is experienced, God's personal presence in our lives is a *sine qua non* for all that follows. Without this fundamental affirmation of the existence of a personal God at the heart of our petitions, we would never find the resources within ourselves to identify our needs and bring them to the Lord. Why would we bother if we did not believe we were actually being heard?

Even this process, however, is not of our own making. Prayer is a gift from God—not the other way around. None of us would be able to pray were it not for the movement of God's grace in our lives. In the words of Saint Alphonsus Liguori, the great Doctor of prayer, "everyone receives sufficient grace to pray" and "if you pray, you will be saved." When we express our needs to God, God is already present in our lives, drawing us toward himself. "Our petition," in the words of the *Catechism*, "is already a turning back to him" (no. 2629). It is a recognition of our limited human nature and a way of expressing our complete and utter dependence on God. Asking for help is also a type of loving ("need love," as C. S. Lewis would say). Those who never ask will never receive and, worse yet, will never find what they are looking for in life.

WHAT TO PRAY FOR

What exactly we ask of God is largely a matter of the quality and intensity of our relationship with him. Jesus' intimate union with the Father led him to pray first for the coming of the kingdom and for the accomplishment of his will, both on earth and in heaven (see Matthew 6:10). Only then did Jesus ask for the more practical things that would sustain him in life and help him extend his healing hand to others. In like manner, the closer we are to God, the more we will identify our needs with those of the kingdom and the more we will pray that his will be done "on earth as in heaven" (Matthew 6:10). This is not to say that we stop focusing on specific needs, but only that we view our asking for them in a different light. There is, in the words of the *Catechism*, a "hierarchy" in our petitions: "we pray first for the Kingdom, then for what is necessary to welcome it and cooperate with its coming" (no. 2632).

As we mature in our relationship with God, perhaps our deepest need is that of becoming more and more open to the Spirit, who helps us in our weakness and intercedes for us as God himself wills (see Romans 8:26–27). In Jesus, God teaches us how to pray; in the Spirit, God actually prays *in us* "...with groanings that cannot be expressed in speech" (Romans 8:26). This groaning in the silence of our hearts gradually rises to the surface of our lives and helps us become more sensitive to the needs of those around us. As the Spirit intercedes for us by praying with us and for us on our behalf, so do we intercede for others by lifting them up to the Lord in prayer. Someone else, in turn, is probably doing the same for us—and we may not even know it! Such is the way of Christian prayer. It makes its way, almost unaware, into the sundry nooks and crannies of daily existence.

Practical Helps

The following practical suggestions are designed to help you get over whatever hesitations you might have about giving your deepest needs and desires to God.

1. Try to get in touch with the various images of God that influence your life of prayer. Special attention should be given to those that promote a dysfunctional way of relating to God. Once those destructive images have been identified, you recognize your need to discard or change them. Ask God for help in this matter and, if necessary, seek the help of a qualified spiritual director. In doing so, past false images (idols?) of God will gradually be cast down and, in turn, you will be able to embrace more readily (and freely) the reality of God's mysterious presence in your life.

2. Moving outward in concentric circles from yourself, to your closest relationships, your faith community, your

environment, your nation, and the world, make a thorough inventory of your various needs. This will help you find perspective in your life and enable you to identify what you most need to pray for. It may also increase your sense of union with the other members of Christ's Body and with the world around you.

3. Now lift all of these needs up to the Lord by praying the Our Father, lingering with the words "Thy kingdom come, Thy will be done on earth as it is in heaven." Once you finish this prayer, continue to allow that particular phrase to resonate in your heart as you reflect upon the various needs you have just lifted up to God. This will help you place the needs you have expressed in the context of the kingdom. By praying for God's will (and not your own) to be done, you humbly recognize your limitations and affirm your radical dependence on God for everything.

4. Give yourself time to rest in silence so that the Spirit has space to move in your life and intercede in your heart before God on your behalf. By allowing the Spirit to yearn within you in this way, you recognize your own inability to pray as you ought. You also allow the Spirit to delve beneath your conscious thought to identify within you and within the Body of Christ all that the community should pray for but has somehow overlooked. This helps you appreciate prayer as something that God accomplishes in you and in the believing community, rather than as a product of your own initiative.

5. Finally, bring your private petitions of prayer to your weekly celebration of the Eucharist. When you join the prayer of a believing community of faith, you bring with you *all* of your needs and place them as one body in the hands of Christ who offers them to the Father in the Spirit.

At the Liturgy, the prayer of the faithful and your praying the Our Father with all those present take on special significance, for this is when you truly pray as a community for the needs of all—including your own. Be grateful for this opportunity.

Conclusion

What are we to make of all this? For some of us, asking for help does not come easy. After all, we live in a society that places a high value on our ability to go it alone, to be self-sufficient—and very often we project this way of interacting with others onto our dealings with God. Some of us do not want to bother God with our needs, either because we are afraid of him or because we do not really believe he cares. Some of us refuse to ask God for help because we do not really think that God has the power to make a difference in our lives, or because we ourselves are too proud to admit that we need a helping hand. Some of us find it hard to conceive of God as a vital, personal presence in our daily lives.

Such problems are by no means insurmountable and, in today's world, they are to be expected. The true test of our character often comes when we face times of difficulty. Those of us who find it hard to open our hearts to God and share with him our deepest needs and desires would do well to focus on the challenge such difficulties present not only to us but also to God. Once we have done so, perhaps the asking will get easier—along with the yearning.

Reflection Questions

1. Do you believe that God cares for you? If so, in what way? from a distance? close up? Do you believe that God would ever give you something that would be harmful to you? If

so, what could that possibly be? If you believe that God truly loves you, why do you fear him?

2. Do you feel comfortable bringing your needs and desires to God? If not, why not? Do you think that God does not hear you or is not interested in you? Do you feel that God has more important things to take of than your measly needs? Who is the God to whom you take your needs and desires?

3. Do you prioritize the things you ask of God? Are some things more important than others? Does your way of prioritizing correspond with Jesus'?

4. Is your petitionary prayer of your own making? Do you bring your needs to God through your own efforts? Does God have any role to play in it? If so, what could it be? If not, then is your prayer a disguised attempt to control God? How do you think God would respond?

5. What role does the Holy Spirit play in the petitions you bring to God? none? a little? a major role? Do you sense the Spirit groaning within you in your private prayer? Do you believe the Holy Spirit is present and intercedes on our behalf when we gather for worship? What do you think the Spirit asks God for each one of us and for the believing community? Do you think God is listening? Do you think God responds?

EXERCISE

Make a list of you needs. Try to be comprehensive, including every aspect of your life: physical, emotional, intellectual, social, and spiritual. When you finish, think of someone close to you and make up a list of that person's needs, again embracing every level of human existence. Do the same for someone you hardly know, perhaps a stranger. When you finish, review your three lists for their similarities and dissimilarities. Try to prioritize the needs you have listed for yourself, putting those that seem the most important at the top of the list and the lesser important ones at the bottom. Do this for the other two lists as well. Then, starting at the top of the lists and making your way to the bottom, bring all of these needs to God. Be sure to mention every need on each list. Do not be afraid to bring even your slightest needs to God, trusting that God will always respond with you best interest in mind.

Book Fifteen

A WALK AT DUSK

Even here, amid the sweep of endless woods,
Blue pomp of lakes, high cliffs and falling floods,
Not undelightful are the simplest charms,
Found by the grassy door of mountain farms.

WILLIAM WORDSWORTH, "AN EVENING WALK"[25]

During the summer months I go to a retreat house in New York's Mid-Hudson Valley, a place situated on 412 acres in the town of Esopus, about eight miles south of the city of Kingston. This quiet spot, snuggled between the majestic waters of the Hudson and the sleepy foothills of the Catskills, holds a special place in my heart. Its commanding view of the river below and the outlying Shaupenaeks to the west give it an atmosphere of rugged containment that I experience nowhere else.

Because roads and footpaths blend into the surrounding woods and meadows without infringing on the area's natural habitat, wildlife abounds in this quiet place. Underground streams surface in unexpected places, offering cool refreshment to the woods' native inhabitants, and towering pines and stately elms provide welcome protection from the summer heat. This land is a walker's paradise, at least to my way of thinking. Through the years, I have especially enjoyed making my way around the grounds at dusk to witness the gradual and unassuming passing of the day.

Rosary Road

I recall one particular evening there, about a year ago. Supper was long over and the cool evening air had finally descended upon the valley. Off to the west, the sun was gradually dipping below the ridge of Sleeping Boy, a distant group of lumbering hills whose shadowy silhouette at twilight, so the townsfolk say, resembles the figure of a slumbering child. As I headed down Rosary Road toward the North Gate for my evening walk, I realized that within the hour the already darkened shapes about me would disappear and all I would be able to discern with certainty would be the swirling dance of stars overhead. I was in no hurry, though; I let each step take its course and was determined to allow things simply to reveal themselves to me as I wondered.

To my right, the monastery that shares the grounds with the retreat house reminded me of the importance of cultivating this contemplative attitude toward life. There, in that quiet hour, I sensed the walls of its cloister resonating with its surrounding world, as if the birds, trees, flowers, grass, deer, mountains, streams, river, and sky were all taking part in the same mysterious dance celebrated by those who lived there. As I continued my walk, I was overcome by a deep sense of gratitude for being able to experience such simple things as the coolness of the evening breeze, the rustling of leaves in trees that lined the road, and the movement of wind through the lower hayfields. For me, the cloister had somehow extended itself in space and I sensed I was walking on sacred ground.

When I came to a wooden bench that overlooked the lower field of wading grass, I sat down for a few minutes to ponder the scene below. Earlier that day, farmers had been harvesting the hay to be used as fodder for their livestock, so the smell of freshly cut alfalfa and timothy filled the air. While swallows flew in formation overhead, performing their synchronized evening ritual, a mockingbird in a nearby oak sang out as if to comment on the swallows' swift and swooping movements. Off to the left, I noticed a solitary robin, no doubt returning from its evening foraging, and a pair of bluebirds circling over their nest in the tall grass. I wondered where they would go once the tractors mowed down the remnants of their tall, grassy refuge.

I imagined the hours ahead: The tranquillity of the moment would gradually fade, twilight would soon pass into night, the quiet of night would give way to the crow of the cock, Sleeping Boy would open his eyes, and the crack of dawn would, once again, descend upon the drowsy inhabitants of the valley. I took in a deep breath and let it out slowly.

When I finally stood up and continued my walk, I caught a glimpse of two young fawns grazing in the grass on the other side of the field. Knowing their mother could not be far away, I slowed my pace to get as close as possible. The darkness was in my favor, so I was able to edge within thirty yards of them. It was then that I noticed the mother, off to the right, looking in my direction with her ears pricked to catch the slightest change in sound. Her lack of motion told me that she was trying to pinpoint my movements. She knew I was there—but she wasn't sure if I knew *she* was there. At my next step, however, she darted across the hayfield into the nearby woods with the two young fawns close behind. Their galloping shapes gradually merged with the shadows and soon disappeared into the mounting darkness.

TO THE RIVER

At the turn in the road, I decided to change my course. Rather than following the paved road to the left, that led to the North Gate, I chose the grassy path to the right, which skirted the southern boundary of the old Pell Farm and eventually joined the road leading to the river. There was nothing profound in my decision to take this "road less traveled"; in fact, I was already a hundred yards down the path before I realized what I had done.

Decisions in life often go that way: We make decisions before we realize we've made them—and then spend much of our time trying to justify them to ourselves and others. I had to smile at how this common human weakness came so vividly to mind during such a leisurely evening walk. I wondered if I myself had acted that way during the past day. If so, I was determined, at least for the moment, to let only my feet do the thinking. Sometimes the best therapy for thought is not to think at all.

When I reached the river, darkness had descended upon the valley and only the light of the moon illumined my surroundings. I walked to the water's edge and heard the waves lapping against the bank. To the right I could make out the dim shape of an old barge, no doubt abandoned years ago. Nothing but an eyesore by day, it now stirred my imagination and led me to ponder the fate of other boats that had navigated this important waterway. This point in the river, I thought, must surely have witnessed many passing vessels. If only its waters could speak, I wondered, what would they say?

Looking downstream, I tried to make out the shoreline of Esopus Island, the small fish-shaped island just to the south that legend attests was one of the landing sites of Saint Isaac Jogues and his companions on their northward missionary journey. Even with the benefit of moonlight, I could not discern its presence so misty was the darkness. Turning my gaze to the water before me, I peered into the stillness of the night and imagined a small band of Indians using the currents of the channel to carry their canoes in silence from their encampment just a few hundred yards upstream. I wondered where they might be going and why they were using the cover of night to serve their purposes. *Esopus*, I am told, is an Indian term meaning, "the land of many waters." The abundance of brooks and streams in the vicinity tell me that these native inhabitants were close to the land and named it well—although I have yet to find the remnants of their campgrounds (and will probably continue my search for some time to come).

A crackling noise in the woods behind me caused me to turn abruptly, but I could not pinpoint its precise location. Whatever it was—a rummaging squirrel, a recluse fox, a foraging deer—it must have been aware of my presence, for the noise ceased and I could hear nothing but the gentle lapping of the water along the river's bank.

Turning back toward the water and peering into its darkness once again, I allowed the stillness to touch the deepest, darkest recesses of my own heart. For the smallest part of a moment, I felt one with the world around me. While eternity flowed before me, I felt as though I were standing outside of it, observing it, watching it run its course. I felt both conditioned by time and yet more than time. Like the river before me, I was caught in the ongoing flow of the Infinite, somehow sure that as my life ran its course, it would somehow empty out into a vast ocean of divine love.

As a sense of awe welled up within me, it felt good to be alive, to breathe, to hear my own heart beat, to know this deep sense of oneness with the universe—to feel somehow more than myself and yet less than myself. In that moment, who I was no longer seemed to matter for, in some small way, I felt bonded with every human breath, every human heartbeat, every movement of human consciousness. What is more, I sensed I was experiencing all of this not just for myself or for humanity, but for all of creation. I was that part of the cosmos looking back at itself, experiencing itself, rejoicing in itself and, in doing so, becoming more than itself, all through the glorious yet elusive influence of God's grace.

THE STATIONS WALK

Coming back to my senses from my momentary lapse of consciousness, I noticed the lateness of the hour and decided that I had better head back toward the retreat house. I took one last look at the dark, flowing water, smiled at the swirling stars overhead, and slowly made my way up the steep road leading back to civilization. Halfway back, I decided to take the footpath that crossed the lower meadow between the retreat house and the river, a path known as the Stations Walk. This short half-mile trail is lined with fourteen wooden posts supporting stone images of the Way of the Cross.

As I made my way, the overhanging branches of the surrounding pines and oaks blocked the light of the moon, so much so that I almost missed the path. The darkness, in fact, was so complete that I could not make out the figures of the stations. When the sound of running water caught my attention, I realized that it was coming from a small brook that fed the pool in the grotto of Our Lady a few yards off to my left. I listened for a few moments and tried to make out the shape of the sheltering stones that protected the statue of Mary, but once again my eyes failed me.

As I continued my walk along this dimly lit path, I sensed how precarious was the walk of faith in the world I inhabit. God was there, but not there; seen, but not seen; present, yet absent to our senses. The way of Jesus, I thought, parallels our own, yet is so very difficult to discern. Darkness prevents us from seeing him, and all we can do is continue our journey, one step at a time, trusting that he is there.

When the path turned at an oblique angle to the right, I found myself in the clearing of the lower meadow, out from the cover of trees. Finally, with the moon and billions of stars providing light, I could see the path and was able to discern the shape of each solitary station. As I drew close to the one nearest me, I reached out and placed my hand on the stone figure of Jesus. For the smallest part of a moment, I felt as though my story and Jesus' had met, that our paths had crossed. Jesus, I thought, must have walked in the darkness and faced the shadows of uncertainty. He must have known the pain of the unknown, the sense of loss over a destiny he no longer controlled. I thought of his agony in the garden, his sweat, his tears. His Father gave him just enough light to take the next step of his journey—no more, no less. In that moment, Jesus seemed so close to me; I could identify more closely with his walk, for I recognized that it was not so very different from my own. I listened to the stillness about me and allowed it to enter me. As I did so, I pondered in my heart the meaning of "the Word made flesh."

As I removed my hand from the stone, I noticed the lights of the retreat house on the other side of the meadow. The retreatants, I thought, would soon be going to bed, continuing their conscious journey in their unconscious dreams of the night. Weariness soon would shut their eyes and lead them into a land of darkness. From where I was standing, I felt strangely at one and at peace with each of them. I prayed for them—strangers to me, but friends all the same—and commended them to God's care.

FINAL STEPS

Slowly, peacefully, I reached the end of the Stations Walk and found myself standing a mere fifty yards from the retreat house. I followed the paved road to the left, circled past the ruins of an old guesthouse, and past the flower bed with the flagpole in the middle and the small statue of Saint Francis at its base. Rather than turning right toward the retreat house, however, something led me to the left, past the tennis courts and playing fields, beyond the apple orchard, to the small cemetery. For a short while I walked among the graves and wondered about those people's lives. How many of them had walked these grounds as I had just done? How many of them were moved by the unexpected noises, the rustling wind, the lapping water, the penetrating darkness? How many of them had walked where I had walked and had come to similar, if not identical, conclusions about the nature of their own uncertainty? I pondered their graves and could see myself in their places, where time itself had not yet led me—but one day surely would.

Hearing the crickets from the lower ponds by the road that led to the South Gate made me feel as though the night were alive with music, the kind of music that caresses the soul and softly lulls a tired child to sleep. By this time, my eyes were growing heavy from the walk, from the deep thoughts, from the mysterious noises of the night. Closing them for a moment, I imagined what the world would have been like without my ever having lived.

As I slowly made my way back to the retreat house, grateful for the passing of the day, for my walk in the twilight, and for the descent of night upon the valley and all who live, rest, and dream there, I realized that the end of my walk was really just the beginning. I came to see that all of my life was like taking a leisurely walk at dusk. As I lay awake in bed later that night, gazing out the window into the deep, impenetrable darkness, I listened happily to the soothing night noises and waited in quiet expectancy for the arrival of sleep—and the mounting shadows of the coming dawn.

Reflection Questions

1. Do you have a routine "winding down" time at the end of your day? If you do not have such a time, do you think you need one? If you do have such a time, what is it like for you? What do you do? How do you let go of the events of the day and prepare yourself for the shadows of sleep and the descent of unconsciousness?

2. Are you an observer? Do you notice what is going on around you? Can you describe in detail, for example, what is going on around you when you go for a walk at night or hold an intimate conversation with a friend? Have you ever tried to give such a description? If so, do you think your description is accurate? How could it be improved?

3. Do you use your imagination? Do you ever let loose your imagination on your surroundings to see where it will take you? Are you threatened by such a suggestion? Does the thought of letting go in this way inspire you or make you fearful? What does imagination have to do with developing a contemplative attitude toward life?

4. Is the narrative of Jesus' passion, death, and Resurrection relevant to your life? Does it give you meaning? Does it help you make sense of your journey through life? Have you ever felt as though Jesus were right beside you, as though his story and yours are not merely parallel but are actually one and the same? If so, how do you interpret this feeling? If not, could you envision this happening to you?

5. What could you do to foster a more contemplative attitude toward your daily life? taking time for quiet throughout the day? being more observant of what is going on around you? seeking the parallels and points of conjunction between your life and that of Jesus? reading sacred Scripture? taking time for prayerful reading? an appropriate combination of any of these? What do you think would best suit you at this particular moment in your life? Can you think of some concrete steps you could take to foster a more contemplative attitude toward your daily life? Would you be willing to take these steps?

EXERCISE

Go for a walk at dusk. If this is not feasible, try to find a secure spot from which you can watch the sunset. As you go about your walk (or watch), keep your eyes on the sun as it goes down on the far western horizon. Be aware of the shadows as they lengthen and gradually turn to darkness. Watch the world as it slowly slips from view and falls asleep. Then close your eyes for a moment. When you open them, imagine Jesus pondering the same sun as it dipped below the horizon so many centuries ago. Look at the dimly lit stars overhead and thank God that your path and Jesus' path have crossed—at least this once. Then ask God to give you the ability to see with the eyes of Jesus, to help you see the rising and setting of the sun each day in the depths of the human heart. When you have finished your prayer, open the Scriptures to Matthew 5:1–12 and read the account of Jesus preaching the beatitudes.

BOOKEND

We become contemplatives
when God discovers Himself in us.
At that moment, the point of our contact
with Him opens out
and we pass through the center
of our own souls,
and enter eternity.

THOMAS MERTON[26]

NOTES

BOOKEND

1. *Seeds of Contemplation* (London: The Catholic Book Club, 1950), 32.

BOOK ONE

2. *The Complete Poems and Plays, 1909–1950.* (New York: Harcourt, Brace & World, Inc., 1962), 124.

BOOK TWO

3. *The Complete Poems of Emily Dickinson*, ed., Thomas H. Johnson (Boston/Toronto: Little Brown and Company, 1960), 691.

BOOK THREE

4. *The Palace of Being: New and Selected Poems* (Chicago: Loyola University Press. 1990), 13.

BOOK FOUR

5. *The Collected Poems of Dylan Thomas* (New York: New Directions, 1957), 61.

BOOK FIVE

6. *A Selection from the Poems of Michael Field* (Boston/New York: Houghton Mifflin Co., 1925), 137.
7. *Thoughts in Solitude* (New York: Farrar, Straus and Giroux, 1958; sixth printing, 1979), 19.

BOOK SIX

8. *Selected Poems of Thomas Merton* (New York: New Directions, 1967), 81.
9. *Thoughts in Solitude,* 18–19.
10. From a flyer of the Monastic Fraternities of Jerusalem. Cited in Henri J. M. Nouwen, *The Road to Daybreak* (New York: Image, 1990), 86.
11. *Thoughts in Solitude*, 20–21.
12. Fyodor Dostoevsky, cited in Frank S. Mead, ed., *The Encyclopedia of Religious Quotations* (New York: Pillar Books, 1976), s.v. "Hell."

13. "The Hollow Men," in *Selected Poems* (New York: Harcourt, Brace & World, 1964), 80.
14. *Sophie's World: A Novel about the History of Philosophy*, trans, Paulette Møller (New York: Farrar, Straus and Giroux, 1994), 152.
15. *Mysticism: A Study and an Anthology* (Harmondsworth, Middlesex, England: Penguin Books, 1963), 121.
16. Anthony de Mello. *One Minute Wisdom* (Anand, India: Gujarat Sahitya Prakash, 1987), 166.

BOOK SEVEN

17. *The Poems of Alice Meynell* (New York: Charles Scribner's Sons, 1923), 112.

BOOK EIGHT

18. *The Oxford Book of English Verse: 1250–1900*, ed., Arthur Quiller-Couch (Oxford: Oxford University Press, 1900), 52.

BOOK NINE

19. *The New Oxford Book of English Verse: 1250–1950*, ed. Helen Gardner (New York/Oxford: Oxford University Press, 1972), 774–75.

BOOK TEN

20. Ibid., 777.

BOOK ELEVEN

21. *95 poems* (New York: Harcourt, Brace, Jovanovich, Inc., 1958), 77.

BOOK TWELVE

22. *The New American Bible*: St. Joseph's Edition (New York: Catholic Book Publishing, Inc., 1970), 670.

BOOK THIRTEEN

23. From *Come Hither: A Collection of Rhymes and Poems for the Young of All Ages,* ed. Walter de la Mare (New York: Alfred A. Knopf, 1957), 640.

BOOK FOURTEEN

24. *The New American Bible*: St. Joseph's Edition (New York: Catholic Book Publishing, Inc., 1970), 12.

BOOK FIFTEEN

25. *Selected Poems and Prefaces*, ed. Jack Stillinger (Boston: Houghton Mifflin Company, 1965), 6.

BOOKEND

26. *Seeds of Contemplation*, 32.